Can D
D1467760

Can Do!

The Story of the Seabees

William Bradford Huie

The War Vault
2020

First printing 2020.

ISBN: **9798616402646.**

Contents

1: History's Greatest Construction War

AS I WRITE THESE WORDS, Allied arms are everywhere on the offensive. We are at last beating at the battlements of Rome. The Red meat chopper is grinding as fine as the mills of the gods, yet faster. Our bombers are spreading a Seversky dreamful of fire over Germany. Britain is stuffed with men ready to leap the Channel. Everywhere there is the feeling that 1944 may see the end of the Hitlerian strut. In the Pacific we are saying, "The Philippines in '44." Resurgent Yankee sea power is daring the Japs to come out and fight. Crumpled Japanese bodies, looking like burnt pieces of celluloid, are as common a sight on our screens as Donald Duck. From China, from the Aleutians, from the Philippines, we are preparing to dump hell's brimstone onto the Sons of Heaven.

How has this miracle been wrought? By what process have we passed from the despair of '42 to the confidence of '44? What sorcery converted the jig-dancing Hitler of Compiègne into the flabby madman crying for St. Helena? Who derailed those White House-bound samurai and set them to carving their own bellies? Whose effort was it that turned the tide?

It is an argument for now and forever. Maybe the tide was turned by those beardless boys who flew the Spitfires over the cliffs of Dover in the fateful fall of '40. Maybe the Beast was hurt most in the rubble of Stalingrad; or maybe his reddest blood was drawn in the sands at Alamein. Some will say that the Beast was smothered in the bloody feather mattress of old China's relentless faith; while others will speak a word for Midway, Bataan, Coral Sea and Guadalcanal. Some will add that perhaps it was the American industrial plant, freedom-built, which really turned the tide.

This argument is good because it will help us to comprehend the enormity of the human effort required to destroy Germany and Japan. True, when we assess the effort we are like the blind men feeling for the elephant; each of us is impressed by the part he feels; but in this war the elephant is so enormous that only by gathering the impressions of many feelers can we hope to realize the enormity of the whole. Germany and Japan have made history's most determined attempt to reinstall the whip as the proper instrument for the government of men; and to defeat this attempt has required the combined strength of all men everywhere who yearn for freedom.

Within our own American ranks the argument as to who "won the war" grows warmer with each new success. Young voices claim that airpower tips the balance; while older voices explain crustily why sea power must decide the issue. Some are certain, as always, that it is the Army infantryman who supplies the difference; while the engineers with their big ears know in their hearts that they are the men amongst the boys. And through it all the Marines quaff their beer, never doubting who does the real fighting.

This intra-American argument, too, is as wholesome as cod liver oil, as rambunctiously American as "Yea, team!" or "Geronimo!" Our fearsome team spirit, nourished from sandlot to college campus to battlefield, is our strength. Each of us insists on contending that his outfit is the "toughest goddamned outfit in the whole goddamned army," and when we add all these boisterous contentions we have the sum of our magnificent effort. Our war machine has so many parts, there are so many specialized organizations within organizations, that we shall need to hear each part extolled before we can comprehend the whole.

In a sense, this narrative is a good-humored entry in the who's-winning-the-war argument. If it convinces you that a hell-roaring Seabee, mounted on a 20-ton bulldozer, will lead the parade through the ruins of Tokyo, then it will have served one of its purposes. It makes no pretense to objective reporting; the author is a Seabee among Seabees, an advocate for his own gang, completely dedicated to the proposition that the Seabees are the goddamnedest, toughest and, withal, most efficient bunch of hairy-chested broncos whoever went to war under the Stars and Stripes.

When a Marine sees a Jap, he shoots the bastard's eyes out; when a Seabee spies a Jap he just spits a long, contemptuous stream of "Copenhagen" and blinds the sonuvabitch!

Seriously, this narrative presents the war as seen and waged by the 8,000 officers of the Navy's Civil Engineer Corps and the 250,000 men of the Naval Construction Battalions. This war is history's greatest air war, greatest sea war, et cetera, and it is also history's greatest construction war.

Before there can be an air war, somebody has got to go somewhere and fight disease, mud and Japs, and build an airstrip. Then the airstrip must have such accouterments as a tank farm to supply fuel, widely dispersed magazines full of bombs and ammunition, gun emplacements to protect it, docks for supply, warehouses, and a complete American community around it. Before PT boats can make their glamorous runs, somebody has got to build a dock and figure out how to lift the boats out of the water and nurse them. The Marines were at Guadalcanal, thank God, but the Seabees were there, too. The Marines did the fighting, and the Seabees had nothing else to do but (1) build and operate Henderson Field; (2) chase Jap bombs and shells around the field and fill up the holes faster than the Japs could blast them; (3) build the docks and unload the ships; (4) cut a few million feet of lumber out of the swamps and convert it into docks, warehouses and barracks; (5) drain the swamps and kill the mosquitoes; and then (6) build a few hundred miles of roads.

The Seabees are the one big, new organization of this war. They were born in the hours of terrible emergency just after Pearl Harbor. Men with a lot of mechanical know-how in their hands had to be rushed to the Pacific islands; men who could fight jungles as well as Japs; men who were accustomed to loneliness and danger; men who could go into battle, if necessary, with little or no military training.

In its desperate crisis, the Navy turned to the nation's natural fighters: to mountain movers who had built Boulder Dam; to sandhogs who had tunneled under East River; to human spiders who had spun a steel web over Golden Gate; to timber-jacks, cat-skinners, dock wallopers; to brawny, loud-cussing, straight-spitting men capable of driving a 10,000-mile road to Tokyo and stamping a few rats along the way.

Few of these men were subject to the draft. Their average age was about thirty-one. They were men with families. Draft deferments and inflated wages in our shipyards and war plants were theirs for the accepting. So, the Navy called for volunteers, and 100,000 of these men volunteered to put on uniforms at service wages within a few months. It was from this cream of America's builders that the first Seabee battalions were formed; and, as rapidly as they could be outfitted, the battalions were rushed to the danger points. The story of how these men have contributed to our victories is as inspiring as any story of the war. You've heard how the war elephant feels to all the glamour boys—the Marines, the PT captains, the Commandos, the submariners, and the hot pilots. Here's how it feels to the Seabees.

A Seabee poses with a highway dedication sign

Bougainville Island, January, 1944

Close-up of sign

2: Men and Mud at Munda

IT WAS A WET DAWN IN THE SOLOMONS. July 1, 1943. D-Day,
H-Hour at Rendova.

Through murky half-light, tropical rain fell in sheets. Heavy,
flat-bellied tank lighters battered down the waves—*krrump,
krrump*—as they pushed from the transports toward East Beach.
In the boats, tight-lipped Seabees, Marines and soldiers (Amphib-
ian Task Force 31, composed of the 24th Naval Construction
Battalion, the Ninth Defense Marines and the 172nd Infantry
Combat Team) crouched by the wet flanks of bulldozers and
watched the palm-fringed beach edge closer. After eleven months
of conquest and consolidation at Guadalcanal, our forces were at
last reaching up the "slot" of the Solomons for the big Jap air
base at Munda on New Georgia Island. From Rendova, Munda
would be within reach of our heavy howitzers.

The high whine of Jap .25-calibers cut across the water as
the bandy-legged rats in the palms began sniping at our coxswains. The men cursed, crouched lower, gripped gun-butts
harder. As though the rain weren't enough, salt water drenched
the men as the boats churned through heavy surf. The boats
skidded in soft sand; ramps dropped; there was a brief, fierce
skirmish; and the Japs who were left alive faded back into the coconut groves. Automatic weapons troops pushed in two hundred
yards to form a defense arc, while the Seabees began furiously
unloading trucks, tractors, heavy guns, ammunition and supplies.

The Jap ground forces had been dispersed easily. Now the
real battle was joined; the battle against nature and time and the
inevitable Jap bombers. Men and supplies are vulnerable while
they are in landing craft; they are even more vulnerable during
the period they are on the open beach. So, in every beach operation the Seabees must drive hard to get ashore; drive even harder
to unload; then exert the last drop of energy to get the supplies
off the beach, dispersed and hidden.

Leading the Seabees was 48-year old Commander H. Roy
Whittaker (Civil Engineer Corps, USNR, Philadelphia, Pa.), a pint-

sized construction veteran with the energy of a jackhammer. He described the action:

"Where we landed the soil was unbelievably marshy," he said. "The mud was deep and getting deeper. A swampy coconut grove lay just back of the beach, and we had to cut road through there. Guns had to be transported from our beach over to West Beach so that shells could be hurled across the narrow strip of water onto the Jap positions at Munda. And still that rain poured.

"All day long we sweated and swore and worked to bring the heavy stuff ashore and hide it from the Jap bombers. Our mesh, designed to 'snowshoe' vehicles over soft mud, failed miserably. Even our biggest tractors bogged down in the muck. The men ceased to look like men; they looked like slimy frogs working in some prehistoric ooze. As they sank to their knees they discarded their clothes. They slung water out of their eyes, cussed their mud-slickened hands, and somehow kept the stuff rolling ashore.

"A detachment under Irv Lee (Lieutenant Irwin W. Lee, CEC, USNR, Monmouth, Ill.) fought to clear the road to West Beach. The ground was so soft that only our biggest cats could get through. The Japs were still sniping, but in spite of this the men began felling the coconut palms, cutting them into twelve-foot lengths and corrugating the road. Our traction-treaded vehicles could go over these logs, but the spinning wheels of a truck would send the logs flying, and the truck would bury itself. To pull the trucks out we lashed a bulldozer to a tree, then dragged the trucks clear with the 'dozer's winch.

"When night came, we had unloaded six ships, but the scene on the beach was dismal. More troops, Marines and Seabees had come in, but the mud was about to lick us. Foxholes filled with water as rapidly as they could be dug. There was almost no place near the beach to set up a shelter tent, so the men rolled their exhausted, mud-covered bodies in tents and slept in the mud. As the Japs would infiltrate during the night, the Army boys holding our line in the grove would kill them with trench knives.

"Next day, at 1330, without warning, the Jap planes came in with bomb bays open. All of us began firing with what guns had been set up, but most of the Seabees had to be in the open on the beach and take it. We tried to dig trenches with our hands and noses while the Japs poured it on us.

"The first bombs found our two main fuel dumps, and we had to be there in the mud and watch our supplies burn while the Japs strafed us. One bomb landed almost under our largest bulldozer, and that big machine just reared up like a stallion and disintegrated. Then every man among us thought that his time had come. A five-ton cache of our dynamite went off, exploding the eardrums of the men nearest it. That soggy earth just quivered like jelly under us.

"When the Japs had exhausted their ammunition they flew off, leaving us to put out the fires and treat our wounded. I'll never forget the scene on that beach. In our outfit, two of our best officers (Lieutenant Lee and Lieutenant George W. Stephenson, CEC, USNR, Klamath Falls, Ore.) and twenty-one men were dead. Many more were wounded, others were missing, and a number were out of their heads. Our galley equipment, most of our supplies, and all the men's sea bags and personal belongings were destroyed.

"'Okay, men,' I yelled. 'We got nothing left but what we got on, so let's get back to work.'

"All that night, Doctor Duryea (Lieutenant Commander Garrett Duryea, Medical Corps, USNR, Glen Cove, N.Y.) worked with our wounded. The biggest job was to get them clean. That's one thing about being a Seabee. Aboard ship you bathe, wash down with antiseptic, and put on clean clothing before an action. In the Air Force you can take a bath before you take off. But when a Seabee gets hit, he's usually on a beach in the mud. Mud seems to be our element. When we die, we die in the mud.

"Next day, while we worked in relays, chaplains from the Army and Marines helped us bury our dead. Three more had died during the night. Not one of those boys would have ever thought of himself as a hero, but I felt proud to have been their commanding officer. They were construction men, most of them from the oil fields of Oklahoma and Texas, and, with never a complaint, they had died in the mud trying their damnedest to get a job done. In any story of the Seabees they deserve to be named.

They were Edgar Barton, Seaman first, Tecumseh, Okla.; William S. Byrd, Machinist's Mate second, Lookeba, Okla.; Robert K. Evans, Chief Carpenter's Mate, Holdenville, Okla.; Charles Gambrell, Seaman first, Vain, Okla.; William P. Rogers, Gunner's Mate first, Wynnewood, Okla.; Tom Thompson, Machinist's Mate second, Oklahoma City; Gustav F. Dresner, Chief Carpenter's Mate, Houston, Tex.; Ralph C. Wendell, Boatswain's Mate second, Rockport, Tex.; Lee Arthur Wilson, Chief Carpenter's Mate, Del Rio, Tex.; George W. Coker, Boatswain's Mate first, Shreveport, La.; William H. Perkins, Shipfitter first, Keithville, La.; Raymond R. Lovelace, Carpenter's Mate first, Martel, Tenn.; Joe Wheeler Plemons, Machinist's Mate first, Harriman, Term.; Robert Dixie Roach, Seaman second, DeQueen, Ark.; Stacy Romine, Seaman second, Menlo, Ga.; Clarence G. Lambesis, Chief Storekeeper, Chicago, Ill.; Max J. Grumbach, Shipfitter third, Hoboken, N.J.; Robert S. Milligan, Storekeeper second, Summit, N.J.; Harold D. Rosendale, Shipfitter first, Sandusky, Ohio; Edward W. Labedz, Seaman first, West New Brighton, N.Y.; Charles H. Long, Fireman first, Flushing, N.Y.; Joseph M. Tabaczynski, Seaman second, Woodbridge, N.Y.; and John M. Young, Shipfitter first, Garden City, N.Y.

"By the morning of the fourth day, we had opened the road to West Beach, but what a road it was! We had literally snaked those big 155's through two miles of mud, and the Marines began setting them up. We were also developing a storage area some distance from the beach and were trying desperately to reduce our hazards on the beach. It takes men with real guts to unload on an open beach without air cover.

"Our men had been under constant strain for ninety hours; at least fifty of them were running high temperatures from constant exposure to mud and water; they could only jump between gasoline drums and powder barrels when the Japs came over; and the beach, as always, was a potential torch with ammunition, diesel oil and gasoline everywhere. The mud was too deep for trucks. To move the inflammable stuff back into the storage areas, the men had to emplace themselves in the mud in bucket-brigade fashion. For hours they'd work that way, passing the heavy packages back into the camouflage area and sinking deeper into the mud each time they handled a package. And still the rain poured.

"Late that afternoon we got our first big thrill. From over on West Beach, the Marines opened up on Munda with the 155's. Our men stopped work and cheered almost insanely. The others stationed with bulldozers and winches along the road to West Beach joined in the cheer. No group of men had ever endured more in order for guns to begin firing. It hurts American construction men down deep to have to lie in mud and be strafed by Japs; and now those 155's were giving it back to the Japs with interest. The firing was a tonic to us. The men went back to unloading furiously.

"We had received some additional equipment, but that night we still had only enough tents and cots for our expanding sick quarters. The men had tried to pitch a few shelter tents, but the tents would sink in the mud. There was still nothing else to do but wrap yourself in whatever you could find and sleep in the mud. When you are sufficiently exhausted you can do that, but after you pass forty you have one helluva time getting up in the morning.

"On the fifth day, we continued to unload troops, supplies and equipment. Our storage areas became more congested, due to our distribution difficulties and also due to delays in transshipments over to our positions on New Georgia Island, from which we were also attacking Munda. The Seabees sent many small working parties to help the Army and Marines, yet our beach condition grew worse under the continuing heavy rains.

At 1400 the Japs bombed us heavily, but this time the damage was much lighter because of the furious anti-aircraft fire.

The Army and Marines had many guns set up by this time, and the Seabees helped man the guns on twenty LSI's [Landing Ship Infantry] and two LST's [Landing Ship, Tank] at the beach. We were able to prevent the Japs from strafing us, and seven Jap planes crashed in our immediate area.

"Seabee casualties were only one man missing and one wounded in this raid, but our number of psychopathic cases had begun to mount. We had to evacuate ten men who had become hysterical. As men grow physically exhausted, they become more and more susceptible to nervous collapse under bombing.

"By the sixth day, the 155's were pouring shells onto Munda almost incessantly, and we still had the supply road open, but our position seemed more impossible than ever. None of us could remember anything except mud and bombs. The rains seemed to get heavier. But somehow the men kept working. Word came that 5,000 troops had been landed on New Georgia near Munda. Munda was doomed if we could just hold out and keep those

155's firing. The Japs knew this as well as we did, so at 1315 they came at us again. But this time it was a different story.

Our own air forces were ready to take up the fight now, and our planes came in and tangled with the Japs right over our heads.

"We lay in those muddy foxholes for an hour and watched the air battle. Since we couldn't fire the AA [anti-aircraft] guns without endangering our own planes, there was nothing else for us to do but lie in our grandstand seats and count the falling Japs. Each time a Zero would burst into flames our exhausted, mud-covered men would leap up and cheer wildly.

"Knowledge that we now had air cover improved our morale on the seventh day. Also, we had managed to borrow three stoves from the Army and Marines and were providing the first hot food for the men. Three air battles were fought over us during the day, but our planes didn't allow the Japs to get close enough either to bomb or strafe us. That night the Japs came over three times, forcing us to hit the water in the foxholes, but most of us had given up hope of ever being dry again,

"On the eighth day we continued to unload supplies, repair landing boats and haul the ammunition through the mud to the 155's. The Marines kept up the shelling of Munda almost continuously. One enemy air attack in the afternoon lasted for fifty minutes, but our planes were opposing the Japs constantly, and we suffered little damage. During the day we evacuated seven additional cases of war hysteria. That night we had to hit the foxholes twice.

"On the ninth day the Japs attempted four large-scale raids, but our damage was slight. Our air cover was now functioning perfectly except at night. We evacuated three more cases of war hysteria, and that night we had to hit the water three times as the Japs bombed us rather heavily. But our bombardment continued, and our roads were still open in spite of the continuing rain.

"On the tenth day we had five light enemy raids, and evacuated additional cases of war hysteria, but morale continued high."

While the 24th Battalion was suffering its long ordeal at Rendova, helping to make possible the shelling of Munda, across forty miles of water, at Segi Point, New Georgia, the 47th Seabee

Battalion was just as furiously playing its role in the Munda drama. The 47th, led by Commander J. S. Lyles (CEC, USNR, Wagoner, Okla.), had been assigned the task of ripping an airstrip out of the jungle so that our bombers coming up from Guadalcanal to bomb Munda could have fighter protection over the target. Success of the whole operation depended on the speed with which this airstrip could be built. The first wave of the 47th began landing at Segi at 1010 on June 30, just twenty hours before the 24th began landing at Rendova.

The landing at Segi had been planned as a sneak operation. It was hoped that the battalion could get ashore unobserved by the Japs and could get a head start on the airstrip before the Japs attacked. To facilitate this strategy, a Seabee scouting party led by Commander Wilfred L. Painter (CEC, USNR, Seattle, Wash.) had slipped ashore from native fishing boats on the night of June 22. The following day Commander Painter selected an abandoned coconut plantation now overgrown with jungle as the site for the airstrip, and the party began laying out the field.

Lieutenant Garland S. Tinsley (CEC, USNR, North Charleston, S.C.) was acting as lookout for the scouting party, and on the second day he saw Japs approaching the shore from two directions. One barge load of Japs landed a mile west of the proposed airfield and two barge loads landed mile and a half east of the field.

Tinsley reported Condition Black, and the party got set for a fight. However, by lying doggo for forty-eight hours, the group eluded the Japs, who took to their barges and disappeared. On D-Day the scouts had the field laid out, ready for work to begin, and they were standing on the beach to direct the landing.

Thanks to this advance survey, when the 47th's big HD-12 bulldozers and power shovels rolled off the boats, they at once began pushing down the coconut palms, clearing the strip. From that moment the 47th battled time and the jungle around the clock. Equipment "unraveled" off the boat as needed. Supplies were unloaded and dispersed. Floodlights were ready before darkness on the first night. A bivouac area was cleared. AA guns were manned; exterior guard posted. And, above all, work proceeded on the airstrip with all possible speed.

Construction of the strip involved the clearing of an initial area of 250 by 3,500 feet; grading and draining the area; covering a minimum area of 100 by 2,500 feet with 12 to 18 inches of coral; and then laying the steel pierced plank, or Marston mat on a minimum surface of 75 by 2,500 feet. This 75 by 2,500-foot space is regarded as the minimum safe surface from which our fighter craft can operate. Our airstrips are thus built in sections, with the aim of producing a minimum "fighter-strip" in the shortest possible time; and then lengthening and widening the strip gradually up to the 300 by 5,000 feet necessary for heavily loaded four-motored bombers.

At 0822 on July 11, the pilot of a Navy Corsair fighter brought his plane down on the strip in an emergency landing which saved both himself and his ship. He pronounced the field ready for use, and the exact time was recorded: 10 days, 22 hours, 12 minutes after the first landing boat had ground ashore! While the Seabees have restored captured Jap fields in much less time, this then stood as the world-record for converting jungle into a landing area.

Amazingly, the Japs did not discover the activity at Segi until the seventh day. This was due both to their preoccupation with our forces at Rendova and to a clever arrangement for handling the lights at Segi. Whenever Jap planes would take off from the Munda field at night, our forces at Rendova would flash the warning to Segi. The 47th would then douse its lights and continue limited construction activities in the dark until Rendova reported that the Japs had returned to Munda.

Here's what the speed record at Segi meant to the Munda operation: It was fighter planes from Segi which helped relieve the Jap aerial pressure on the men-in-the-mud at Rendova. The Segi fighters stood at Ready Alert, and when our bombers came up from Guadalcanal to bomb Munda, the Segi fighters roared into the air to escort the bombers over the target. Conversely, it was the Seabees, Marines and soldiers on Rendova who, with their shelling, so monopolized the attention of the Japs that the 47th had their field virtually completed before the Japs found it.

"When the Japs did discover us," Commander Lyles reported, "we got a severe pounding. They hit a dynamite dump, one of our fuel dumps, and peppered our bulldozers and trucks with shrapnel. But they arrived too late with too little.

"In at least one way the Japs helped us set our record. On our fifth day we got the news that twenty-three Seabees had been killed over at Rendova. Our men redoubled their efforts. Many of them insisted on working eighteen-hour stretches in order to rush the air cover."

During the eleven days in which the 47th was setting its record, 14 inches of rain fell at Segi Point!

Three weeks after the opening of the airstrip at Segi, the last Jap had been killed at Munda. On August 9, 1943, advanced platoons of the 73rd Seabee Battalion began work on the blasted Jap air base. The Japs had been unable to operate the field for eight weeks, but Commander Kendrick Podone (CEC, USNR, Forest Hills, N.Y.), leader of the 73rd, was ordered to have the field in operation by August 18.

On August 11, additional units of the 73rd arrived, and Commander Doane ordered round-the-clock operations. The weather gods smiled at last, and a full moon came out to make artificial lighting unnecessary. In just two more days, the men had repaired the north and south runways, and American planes began landing at Munda on the afternoon of August 13. During that night the battalion completed additional hardstands off the runways, and on the 14th the field received forty-eight additional planes.

On August 15, the 24th Battalion, which had fought the mud battle at Rendova, arrived at Munda; and the two battalions set to work to make Munda a major base. The Japs had dug an elaborate tunnel system in the coral, and many of them had died in the tunnels from our flamethrowers. The Seabees cleaned out the Japs and converted the tunnels into deluxe living quarters where a man could sleep and never have to jump up and run for a foxhole.

In November 1943, Admiral Bill Halsey declared that Munda was the finest air base in the South Pacific. A citation for Commander Doane read, in part:

PRIOR TO HIS COMMENCING WORK AT MUNDA THERE WERE NO ROADS, AND THE AIRFIELD AND TAXIWAYS WERE UNUSABLE DUE TO THE BOMBARDMENT AND SHELLING OF THE AREA BY OUR FORCES PRIOR TO ITS CAPTURE. IN SPITE OF SHORTAGE OF PERSONNEL AND EQUIPMENT, AND FACED WITH A TASK OF GREAT

MAGNITUDE, COMMANDER DOANE WAS ABLE, NEVERTHELESS, BY VIRTUE OF HIS PLANNING, LEADERSHIP, INDUSTRY, AND WORKING "ROUND THE CLOCK" TO MAKE SERVICEABLE THE MUNDA AIRFIELD ON AUGUST 14TH, 1943, A GOOD FOUR DAYS AHEAD OF THE ORIGINAL SCHEDULE.

THOUGH SUBJECTED TO SHELLING AND BOMBING, BOTH IN THE CAMP AREA AND ON THE AIRFIELD, COMMANDER DOANE AND HIS MEN HAVE EXPANDED THE SIZE AND FACILITIES OF THE AIRFIELD AT A PHENOMENAL RATE. IN ADDITION, THE ALL-WEATHER ROAD NET AND THE AIR HOUSING AREA HAVE BEEN COMPLETED FAR FASTER THAN HAD BEEN HOPED.

On receipt of his citation, Commander Doane commented: "It's easy to perform construction miracles with men like the Seabees. They are the world's finest construction men. Courage is innate with them. They volunteered to do a job, and all they want is a chance to finish that job as soon as possible. When we took men like this and put them into one organization, we loaded the dice against the Japs."

Commander Doane failed to mention one other factor which contributed to Seabee success at Munda. He himself had built a few airfields before he got to Munda. One of them which he helped to plan and superintend is LaGuardia Field, New York. And Commander Lyles, who set the record at Segi Point, built the Will Rogers Airport at Oklahoma City.

Bill "Bull" Halsey—Fleet Admiral William Frederick Halsey Jr., KBE
(October 30, 1882 – August 16, 1959)

3: Can Do at Guadalcanal

THE SEABEE STORY OF GUADALCANAL BEGINS on the afternoon of August 20, 1942, when wiry, 45-year-old Commander Joseph P. Blundon (CEC, USNR, Keyser, W. Va.) arrived in a PBY off Lunga Point and promptly reported to General A. A. Vandegrift of the Marines. Like many Seabee officers, Commander Blundon saw service in World War I with the Army Engineers. He left his private engineering business to join the Seabees because he "wanted a little excitement" and because his only son was not yet old enough to volunteer. He is a graduate of Maryland Agricultural College and Cornell.

"I guess I was the first Seabee to go under fire," Commander Blundon recalled. "The Marines had been on Guadalcanal thirteen days, and they had a tiny beachhead around Henderson Field. While I was reporting to General Vandegrift, the Jap bombers came over and I hit my first foxhole. I just lay there and trembled with patriotism while the bombs fell around us.

"A few days later, my Sixth Seabee Battalion arrived, and we assumed full responsibility for the completion and maintenance of Henderson Field. The Japs had cleared an area 300 by 5,600 feet, but it was by no means finished. Two 1,800-foot sections at the ends of this area had been graded, and while these sections were rough, our fighters could operate off of them. In the gap between the graded sections about 1,000 feet more had been partially graded, and the remaining 1,000 feet had not been graded at all. The Japs were shelling the field with howitzers, as well as bombing it night and day; and it was our job to keep the holes filled up while we finished the grading, laid the Marston mat, built hardstands and revetments, and helped solve the fuel and ammunition problems.

"We had very little equipment. We had one carryall—the big, waddling machine that scoops up twelve cubic yards of earth—two bulldozers, six dump trucks, twenty-five flat-bottom Jap trucks, one motor patrol grader, one Jap tractor, and one Jap sheeps-foot roller. We also had 10,000 barrels of Jap cement, 18,000 feet of Jap soil pipe, plenty of Jap creosoted poles and a supply of Jap lumber. This Jap material and equipment saved our skins.

'The men in our battalion had not been together more than ten days before we left the States. We had been given our medical shots, a little hasty military indoctrination, and then we had been formed into a battalion and rushed to the South Pacific. We didn't kid ourselves. We weren't a trained military organization; we were just 1,100 partially armed civilians. We had one '03 rifle for each two men. That was all that could be spared us. But all of us were experienced construction men. We knew the value of teamwork. We knew how to take orders; and, more important, we knew how to execute orders. General Vandegrift assigned us a section of the beach to defend against Jap landings, and we figured we could defend that beach and still do the job at Henderson Field.

"We realized at the outset that the battle was going to turn on how fast we filled up holes and how fast we could develop that field. When the Jap bombers approached, our fighters took off; the bombers blasted the airstrips; and then if we couldn't fill up those holes before our planes ran out of fuel, the planes would have to attempt to land anyway, and they would crash. I saw seven of our fighters crack up in one bitter afternoon. From our point of view, the battle of Guadalcanal was a race between the Jap artillery and air force and the Sixth Seabee Battalion.

"We played our cards fast. We pitched our camp at the edge of the field to save time. We dug our foxholes right up alongside the landing area. We found that a 500-pound bomb would tear up 1,600 square feet of Marston mat, so we placed packages of this quantity of mat along the strip, like extra rails along a railroad. We figured out how much sand and gravel were required to fill the average bomb or shell crater, and we loaded these measured amounts on trucks and placed the trucks under cover at strategic points. We had compressors and pneumatic hammers to pack the fill into the craters. We organized human assembly lines for passing up the pierced plank and laying it.

"Then when the Jap bombers approached, every Seabee, including even our cooks, manned his repair station. Our crater crews were lying in the foxholes right at the edge of the strip. The moment the bombers had passed over, these men boiled out of the holes and raced for the craters. While they were tearing away the twisted steel plank, our trucks roared out of hiding to dump their earth and gravel into the holes. The men with the compressors and pneumatic hammers leaped into the holes and began packing the dirt as it came in. Our human assembly lines began passing in the new steel plank and laying it. Every man had to keep his eyes peeled for Jap strafing planes, and when the Jap dived in, our men dived for the close-at-hand foxholes. The men who were working in the crater just used the crater as protection against the strafers.

"We found that 100 Seabees could repair the damage of a 500-pound bomb hit on an airstrip in forty minutes, including the replacing of the Marston mat. In other words, forty minutes after that bomb exploded, you couldn't tell that the airstrip had ever been hit. But we needed all of this speed and more. In twenty-four hours on October 13 and 14, fifty-three bombs and shells hit the Henderson airstrip! During one hour on the 14th we filled thirteen bomb craters while our planes circled around overhead waiting to land. We got no food during that period because our cooks were all busy passing up the steel plank. There were not enough shovels to go around, so some of our men used their helmets to scoop up earth and carry it to the bomb craters. In the period from September 1 to November 18, we had 140 Jap raids in which the strip was hit at least once.

"Our worst moments were when a Jap bomb or shell failed to explode when it hit. It still tore up our mat, and it had to come out. When you see men choke down their fear and dive in after an unexploded bomb so that our planes can land safely, a lump comes in your throat and you know why America wins wars.

"Shell craters are more dangerous to work on than bomb craters. You have a feeling that no two bombs ever hit in the same place; but this isn't true of shells. A Jap five-inch gun lobs a shell over on your airstrip and blasts a helluva hole. What are you going to do? You know, just as that Jap artilleryman knows, that if he leaves his gun in the same position and fires another shell, the second shell will hit in almost the same spot as the first one. So, a good old Jap trick was to give us just enough time to start repairing the hole and then fire the second shell. All you can do is depend on hearing that second shell coming and hope you can scramble far enough away before it explodes. But this is a gamble which is frowned upon by life insurance companies.

"Al Pratt (Lieutenant Alma P. Pratt, CEC, USNR, Fort Duchesne, Utah) was in direct charge of the crater-filling crews. He was an earth-moving specialist; a stocky, serious-minded fellow who recovered quickly from any shock. One afternoon Jap artillery had chased him all over the strip. He'd been knocked down twice by those 'second shell' bursts, he was groggy and very dirty, yet he was still charging upend down the strip, bellowing for more speed.

"In addition to our crater-filling efforts, we fought the Japs by working constantly to enlarge the operating surface of the field. Fighter planes can take off and land safely on a steel-matted area of 75 by 2500 feet. So, when we finished an area 150 by 2500 feet, we had what amounted to two operating strips; since if we had craters on one side of this area we could rope off the damaged side and use the seventy-five-foot-wide strip that was not damaged. Then, when we finally completed an area 150 by 5,600 feet, we had four fighter strips. With the larger area we still had only one safe bomber strip, but bombers carry so much more fuel than fighters that they can give you more time to make repairs.

"Several times in the early days before we got the field lighted we had to land planes after dark. In such emergencies Seabees would hold flashlights and form a human boundary around the landing strip. Death would literally hover over these men, since the planes, often partially out of control, would come in feeling their way, and if they caught a little air pocket even the brush of a wingtip would sever the head of any man holding a light.

"In spite of all our speed, however, I think we might have lost that fight had it not been for the emergency strip which we roughed out early in September. The Japs didn't discover we had this strip for a long time, and the stories I've seen about Guadalcanal don't even mention it. Yet we had it, and I think it saved the show for us.

"This strip was about 2000 feet from the Henderson strip and ran parallel to Henderson. At the start it was nothing more than a sage-grass field with the grass eight to ten feet high. We went in there with machetes and cut the grass off to about eighteen inches high. Then we rolled the grass down, filled in the depressions, and we had a strip which was rough, but one which we used on plenty of occasions when we had more holes than we could fill on Henderson. Even B-17's could get down and get off on this grass in extreme emergency.

"In the final analysis, of course, it was the quality of the men of the Sixth Battalion which enabled us to win the airfield battle. All of them had volunteered for front-line work and that's very important. Less than 10 per cent of them proved unfit for duty under bombs. Compared to any outfit in the service, that's a low percentage. A few men just couldn't take it, but we weeded them out quickly. I think their number was miraculously low in view of the fact that we had had no realistic military training and very little training of any sort.

"The average age of the men was about thirty-five. Many of us were old enough to have been the fathers of the Marines who did the fighting. But I regard this as an advantage rather than a disadvantage. I think the older men stood up better under bombing than the younger men. The man of thirty-eight who has spent his life in active construction work is tough. He doesn't have the physical stamina of the boy of eighteen; he's not as reckless. But when the chips really go down and a job has got to be done, I'll take the experienced, level-headed man of thirty-eight.

"In our part of this war, it's experience and know-how that count. A man may be strong as a bull and ferocious as a tiger, but his hands must be skilled for the Seabees are the men who use America's machines to advantage. One skilled Seabee operating a twelve-cubic-yard carry-all can move as much dirt in eight hours as 150 Jap laborers. To repair the same bomb crater that we can repair in forty minutes takes the Japs three hours, and then they only fill the hole with dirt. They have no compressors or pneumatic hammers, and they have no steel mat.

"As a fighting man, either on the ground or in the air, the Jap is outmatched by the American. But the Jap is a capable, determined fighter, and he can give a good account of himself against the American. But when it comes to military construction, the Jap is hopelessly outclassed. While America has been building super-highways, skyscrapers and TVA's, the Japs have been building dog trails and fiber huts. As a fighting man, perhaps the Jap merits some respect from us; but as a construction man the Jap merits only the contempt which the Seabees have for him."

"Dune" Gillis (Duncan James Gillis, Shipfitter first, Detroit, Mich.) has a pair of confident brown eyes set in a weather-beaten face. Born in Nova Scotia thirty-seven years ago, he has the hard, capable hands of a man who knows ships and docks. When the heat was on at Henderson Field, he ran a power shovel. Then, on other days, he helped operate pontoon barges between ships and the shore at Guadalcanal. Dune Gillis is the kind of Seabee who can do damn near anything.

"You want to know how I got the Silver Star?" Dune asked. "Well, it wasn't much. A lot of fellows deserved it more than I did. It was on the thirteenth of October, and we had had a heavy day of bombing from daylight to dark. I was in a little shallow foxhole up close to the strip at Henderson Field. We had been jumping out and filling up the holes in the main runway. It was about 2300, and Jap warships had begun shelling us. The way the shells were coming in we figured there must be a battleship set-ting offshore, and between the shells and the rain it was one helluva mess. Those big 14-inch babies would come whistling in, go off, and you'd rattle around in your foxhole like a ping-pong ball.

"Well, I was lying in this little shallow foxhole, but right close by there was a big foxhole with eight men in it. And just about then I was thinking maybe I had rather go over and be with them because it gets mighty scary when you are sitting in a hole by yourself with those shells whizzing through the air. The Japs would give us the starboard guns for about an hour, then turn in a circle and give us the port guns. After one salvo when I figured it was about time for the Japs to turn around again, I put my head up for air. I heard a call for help. My buddy, Osborn (How-ard L. Osborn, Shipfitter first, Dearborn, Mich.), who also received the Silver Star, was in a foxhole not far from me. It was awfully dark. You couldn't see anything. But Osborn yelled: 'Let's go, Dune!'

"There were five other fellows close by. The seven of us crawled over to the big foxhole which I had intended to get in and found that a shell had closed it up and trapped all the fellows. The seven of us started digging these men out. We got five out in a hurry, then the shelling started again, and the fellows who were helping me and Osborn ran back to their holes. Osborn and I were kind of crazy, but I'll always remember what he said: "I'm still with you, Dune."

"This was all located in a coconut grove, and trees were every which way, and dirt and mud scattered all over. The foxhole where those fellows were caught was six feet deep, eight feet long and four feet wide. Thompson was in one end and Ward and Carlisle were in the other, and we couldn't use shovels because it was too much of a mess. So, we used our helmets and our hands. The shelling was shaking hell out of us, but by this time we were working too fast to care. We pulled Ward out (Henry L. Ward, Quartermaster first, Port Arkansas, Tex.); he was stuck clear up to his armpits. We laid him aside and started pulling Carlisle out (Wayman M. Carlisle, Carpenter's Mate first, Morning View, Ky.). His head was just barely showing. He finally recovered. And Thompson (Henry L. Thompson, Machinist's Mate first, Chariton, Iowa)—we found him, and he was sitting down. That is, he was at the bottom of the foxhole next to where the shell had hit. He was dead, but the concussion had probably killed him anyway.

"The shelling lasted almost four hours, and the hit that covered these men came about midway. But, believe me, we were still digging, trying to get those men out, when it was over. That's what they gave me and Osborn the Silver Star for.

"And the Purple Heart? You want to know how I got the Purple Heart? Well, that's a story that involves Bucky Meyer (Lawrence C. Meyer, Seaman first, Toledo, Ohio). Our camp was at the edge of Fighter Strip No.1. There was a dugout near the main runway, and this was where Bucky Meyer hung out. He had salvaged a .30-caliber machine gun, had cleaned it and set it up in his dugout. I helped him get some ammunition from the Marines.

"Bucky was always so appreciative of anything that was done for him. He and I stood guard a lot and he always told me stories about his dad; how they liked the outdoors and "fishing and hunting." In those days Henderson Field was a twenty-four-hour proposition for us. I mean we were grading and filling holes and driving trucks all the time. On the third of October, the Japs had been strafing us so bad we could hardly work. And Bucky was itching for a Zero to come up close enough for him to use his gun. Finally, a Zero came right in over us. As the alarm had started sounding, Bucky had jumped off his truck and started full speed for that gun. I jumped off my bulldozer and into a ditch. Quite a few bullets hit Bucky's truck, but he wasn't in it. Just goes to show that when your number isn't up they can't get you.

"Well, that Zero came in about 200 feet from the ground, just shooting like all hell. But Bucky had reached his gun and was firing back for all he was worth. We saw Bucky's tracers hitting the Jap, and we all yelled for him to keep it up. The Jap went down in flames right at the end of the strip. We got several Jap planes that day, and the Seabees got at least one of them.

"A few days later, on October 16, just three days after the shelling in which I was cited for the Silver Star, we were told that the destroyer *McFarland* would run in that night with a load of aviation gas. Me and Bucky and sixteen other Seabees were ordered to take a pontoon barge out to meet the Mack. We tied up alongside the Mack and had taken 350 drums of gas aboard when the Jap planes started coming in.

"The officer aboard the Mack ordered us to stand by to cast off. We were tied up alongside the Mack's port side, and I was next to the ship handling one of the lines. Bucky was over on the sea side of the barge—always ready for anything. I had had four turns around the stanchion, and I had cast off three turns and was ready to let her go. The first plane dropped her bombs and missed us completely, but the second plane got the Mack. The bomb exploded the depth charges which blew off the Mack's stern.

"By this time, we had cast off and had started to drift. Then everything went black for me. There were two hits on the barge, and like most of the other seventeen Seabees, I was blown into the water by the concussion. I was picked up pretty soon, but some of our fellows weren't found for twenty-four hours. Bucky Meyer and seven other Seabees were killed, but ten of us came out alive. They picked shrapnel out of me for a week and found that my eardrums were ruptured, but otherwise I wasn't hurt. The hospital was in a nice coconut grove, and they did the best they could for us. That's how I got the Purple Heart, but I always hated that Bucky got killed before he even knew that he had been awarded the Silver Star for shooting down that Jap."

The seven other men killed with Bucky Meyer on the barge were: Raleigh B. Jennings, Chief Shipfitter, Van Nuys, Cal; J. Alfred Addor, Carpenter's Mate second, St. Louis, Mo.; Jack L. Brinker, Carpenter's Mate third, Grabill, Ind.; Joseph A. Deeks, Carpenter's Mate second, Westlake, Ohio; Edwin B. Janney, Seaman second, Toledo, Ohio; Herluf V. Jensen, Shipfitter second,

Kimballton, Iowa; and Justin J. Plas, Seaman second, of Elyria, Ohio.

Because Bucky Meyer was the first of a number of Seabees to win the Silver Star for gallantry, here is the citation read by the Secretary of the Navy to Bucky's wife, Mrs. Jean Meyer, 121 Segur St., Toledo:

> FOR CONSPICUOUS GALLANTRY AND INTREPIDITY DURING ACTION AGAINST ENEMY JAPANESE FORCES IN THE SOLOMON ISLANDS, OCTOBER 3, 1942. WHILE WORKING ON CONSTRUCTION AND MAINTENANCE OF AN AIRFIELD, MEYER MANNED A MACHINE GUN MOUNTED IN A PIT WHERE HE HAD TAKEN SHELTER DURING AN AIR-RAID ALARM.
>
> ACTING UNHESITATINGLY AND BEYOND THE CALL OF REGULAR DUTY, HE FIRED ON ENEMY ZEROS DURING THE JAPANESE STRAFING ATTACK WHICH FOLLOWED, AND IT WAS OBSERVED THAT TRACER BULLETS FROM HIS GUN REPEATEDLY STRUCK AN ENEMY PLANE WHICH WAS SHOT DOWN.
>
> ON OCTOBER 16, 1942, HE WAS KILLED IN ACTION WHILE WORKING ON A PONTOON BARGE LOADED WITH GASOLINE WHICH WAS STRUCK BY AN ENEMY BOMB. HE GALLANTLY GAVE UP HIS LIFE IN THE SERVICE OF HIS COUNTRY.

Whereupon the Secretary of the Navy presented Mrs. Meyer both the Silver Star and the Purple Heart.

On November 1, 1942, the 14th Seabee Battalion landed at Koli Point, Guadalcanal, and began developing the second camp area on that strategic, ninety-mile-long island. Koli Point is about twelve miles from Henderson Field. The 14th was commanded by Commander Thomas F. Reilly, Jr. (CEC, USNR, West New Brighton, N.Y.), who was a private in the Army Engineers in the last war and who for many years has directed city engineering projects on Staten Island.

Then, in December 1942, Commander Blundon's Sixth Battalion was moved to New Zealand for a rest, and the Sixth was replaced in the Henderson Field area by the 26th Battalion. The 26th was led by Commander C. A. Frye (CEC, USNR, Tulsa, Okla.). It was in contact with the enemy during the six weeks when the Japs made their last bitter attempts to save face.

The story of 26-year-old George T. Wendelken, Fireman first, of New York City, is a part of the record of the 26th. Wendelken is a husky, red-haired, freckled-faced Seabee who in 1925 and '26 played the role of Freckles in Hal Roach's "Our Gang" comedies. After three adventuresome years in the Merchant Marines, he had joined the Seabees because he thought they would give him the fastest action. He was awarded the Purple Heart for a nightmarish experience.

"We landed the day after Christmas with the Sixth and 10th Marines," he explained, "and the Japs welcomed us with a bombing raid. In fact, the Japs had driven us off three times before our ships could pull in close enough for us to take to the landing boats. The 26th encamped at the edge of Henderson Field where the Sixth had been. The Japs were now centering their fire on the Seabee quarters. They had learned that it didn't do them any good to blast the airfield as long as Seabees were on hand to repair it, so now they were concentrating on Seabees.

"We met this threat by digging even more deluxe foxholes than the Sixth had left. These holes would protect us from anything except a direct hit; and nobody worries about a direct hit because if you get one you never know it. My foxhole was forty feet from my tent, but I could roll out of my sack and hit it in exactly three steps when that 'Condition Red' sounded.

"One night in January my number came up. I dived for that foxhole, and then blacked out cold. Next morning at ten o'clock the corpsmen found me. Three officers and eighteen men were dead in nearby holes, but seven other chaps and myself were still alive. The bomb must have been a thousand-pounder. Then began the most fearful fifteen days of my life. Bomb fragments had torn hell out of both my legs, and I was paralyzed from my hips down. We were in the midst of our final offensive, and the Japs were saving face by bombing us around the clock.

"The doctors decided that a foxhole was the safest place for me, so I lay in a foxhole for fifteen days and nights. At intervals the corpsmen would feed me plasma and glucose. On the eighth day the Security Officer brought me a rifle and some ammunition. 'We are expecting an imminent counter-invasion,' he said. 'A huge Jap task force has been spotted up north and may be headed for here. We can't evacuate you, because there are too many wounded to be gotten out. If the Japs break through and get this far, get as many as you can and God bless you.'

"Well, I lay there with my rifle and prayed. The Seabees were preparing to defend Red Beach—a hotspot. Our long-range bombers were taking off to try to disperse the Jap task force, and I looked up at those bombers and prayed for their success. My foxhole just happened to be placed so that when I looked up I could see that black flag waving, meaning Condition Black: Invasion Expected. Nothing depressed me like that flag. I was getting weaker all the time, but I determined to get a few Japs before I passed out. On the twelfth day, however, I was so weak that the corpsmen gave me up. A chaplain came around and prepared me for death, and since the Japs were coming anyway, there didn't seem to be much reason for holding on. But when the news came that the Jap convoy had been dispersed, I seemed to gather a little strength. On the sixteenth day I was moved out of the foxhole to be evacuated in a DC-3 transport.

"There were three transports going out and I was told that would be placed on the first one, but when the litter bearers carried me up to the plane it was full, and I had to wait for the next plane. That was another break. The first plane was shot down by the Japs. I got the last place aboard the second plane, and we started on the 700-mile trip back to the New Hebrides. The plane was an ordinary commercial plane without a gun on it, and if an engine failed or the Japs attacked, we didn't have a chance.

"On the way we got word that the Japs were attacking the cruiser *Chicago* and the destroyer *DeHaven* which lay in our path. We were ordered to head for the clouds, and by hiding and zigging and zagging we somehow got through. The Japs got both of the ships, as well as both the other planes loaded with wounded.

"While I was in the foxhole I had contracted malaria along with my other troubles, so I was sent on down to New Zealand. I had dropped off from 168 to 118 pounds, and I was still living on glucose and plasma. Once again, the corpsmen gave me up and I was supposed to die, but unless your number is up all hell can't kill you. I had seven sieges of malaria before I could get out of that hospital, but I beat the rap and had the sweet privilege of laying my eyes on these United States again."

Just as the geese saved Rome, so the parrots, according to the Seabees, saved Guadalcanal.

The Seabees had a coral pit from which they dug coral for road building. One day a crew of fifteen men were in the pit loading trucks. During a lull between trucks the men crawled up on the edge of the pit and one of them began pot-shooting at the parrots up on the ridge, while the others razzed him about his misses. Suddenly they all went bug-eyed and dived back into the pit.

The parrots were returning the fire!

A large patrol of Japs had infiltrated, and they were holed up waiting for darkness, when they could slip down to the airstrip and dynamite our planes. When the Seabee began firing toward the ridge, he luckily had fired straight toward the Jap hiding places; so, the Japs, assuming they had been discovered, immediately set up a machine gun and returned the fire.

The Japs were well entrenched, and so tightly did their guns cover the coral pit that it was two days before the Seabees could get out. Finally, old Lew Diamond, the indestructible Marine mortar expert, had to come up and blast the Japs out of their position.

Except for the lucky shots which caused the Japs to betray their presence, many of our planes might have been destroyed.

In the months that followed the completion of our conquest of Guadalcanal, Seabee battalions converted the Henderson Field and Koli Point areas into a vast base of operations for all American arms. First came all the vital construction. Great tank farms with miles of pipelines to fuel both aerial and naval thrusts at the enemy. Ammunition magazines widely dispersed and camouflaged, with interlacing roads. Docks over which mountains of supplies could move to the acres of warehouses and storage areas. And the airfields became far more than the minimum operating areas which the Sixth Battalion had fought so courageously to expand and to keep in repair. Hardstands, the hardsurfaced parking areas for planes, became so numerous around the runways that the whole area resembled a vast honeycomb. Around the hardstands, revetments were built to protect the parked planes from bombs and shrapnel.

Then all the American facilities for human existence began to take shape. Spacious dining halls, comfortable barracks, artistic chapels, telephones, radios, electricity, plumbing, movie houses, reading rooms, basketball courts—the Seabees brought all of these to a jungle island. One battalion built a narrow-gauge railroad to connect the docks with the warehouses. The Tojo Ice Plant began to produce tons of ice for the big hospitals and the soft-drink dispensaries.

It was the Marines and the Army who drove the Japs off Guadalcanal, but it was the Seabees who brought America to the island.

Many battalions had a part in the evolution of the island from jungle to modern American military community. The Sixth and the 14th were the pioneers, followed closely by the 26th, then came the 18th, led by Commander L. E. Tull (CEC, USNR, Washington, D.C); the 27th, by Lieutenant Commander W. G. Triest (CEC, USNR, New York City); the 61st, by Commander B. M. Bowker (CEC, USNR, Jacksonville, Fla.); the 63rd, by Commander Frank Highleyman (CEC, USNR, Ogallala, Neb.); and the 46th, by Commander P. F. Henderson (CEC, USNR, Los Angeles, Cal.).

As the base developed, the Seabees on Guadalcanal were organized into the 18th Naval Construction Regiment, which was headed by Commander W. W. Studdert (CEC, USNR, Midland, Tex.). Then, more recently, as the work has been completed and only maintenance has become necessary, the full 1,100-man battalions have been gradually displaced by the smaller Construction Battalion Maintenance Units. Many other battalions have used Guadalcanal as a staging base, but the ones mentioned above deserve the credit for the remarkable transfiguration of the island. As will be explained subsequently, the stevedore battalions were a later development in the Seabees. They were formed to relieve the unloading bottleneck in the Pacific, to speed up the turn-round of ships.

At the risk of becoming too technical, I am going to include a story told me by Commander Frye of the 26th Seabee Battalion. His report, covering one year of operations in the Solomons, shows the interested layman just how complex modern warfare is, and it explains more clearly than any editorial just why the Pacific war must move slowly. I have chosen the 26th Battalion only because it is typical of the 150 construction battalions which are now projecting American know-how to our advance bases.

In analyzing this report, bear in mind that this is the year's work of only one of twelve Seabee battalions which have worked on one island in the Solomons. The eleven other battalions did comparable amounts of work, and Army and Marine engineering units also made contributions. Then you will have some idea of what it means to build a military road across the Pacific Ocean.

"Our battalion landed at Guadalcanal on December 26,1942," Commander Frye said, "and was in ground contact with the enemy until February 9, 1943. The tour of duty was completed December 5, 1943. Construction work was underway every day during this period.

"In contrast to the manner in which most battalions are equipped at present, the 26th landed with no construction material and with only eight jeeps to serve for both our transportation and construction equipment. Due to the exigencies of war very little of the construction material and only a fraction of the equipment originally assigned to us ever arrived, and this came several months after the arrival of the battalion. We took over the limited and badly worn equipment of the Sixth Battalion, and with this equipment, supplemented by captured Japanese and shop-made equipment, the battalion successfully carried out an extensive and varied program.

"Among the outstanding performances of this battalion are:

The construction and maintenance of 35.5 miles of three- and four-lane roads and 21 miles of secondary roads. Much of this road was built through swamp and jungle within enemy artillery and sniper range and during periods of consistent enemy bombing. During critical period two miles of this road approaching the Matanikau River were built in one week. The river was bridged, and jeep roads pushed up to the front lines.

In addition to grading the roads, we also graded a 50-acre area for the Service Command Supply Dump, three acres for the Navy Salvage Dump, and a large LST landing area, and moved 6,500 yards of earth to cover torpedo and ordnance magazines.

We constructed and maintained eleven new bridges totaling 1,136 lineal feet. We also rebuilt three bridges after flood damage, and redecked five major bridges. We manufactured 9,603 lineal feet of culvert from discarded oil drums and used it in highway construction. We loaded and hauled 191,423 cubic yards of gravel and 88,990 cubic yards of coral.

The battalion built seven docks of various sizes. Practically all hardware for these structures was shop-fabricated from Japanese steel. We built a 180-foot Marine railway for beaching tank lighters and poured 100 concrete anchors complete with eye bolt and three feet of chain.

We completed 55,750 barrels of storage capacity for gasoline and fuel oil, and 27,000 feet of pipeline. We handled a total of 84, 269, 043 gallons of aviation gasoline without an accident or delay in getting planes into the air. One of our improvements in the technique of handling aviation gasoline enabled us to increase the speed of this operation from 3,300 gallons per hour to 9,900 gallons per hour. We were commended both for this improvement and for our expeditious service on an Aircraft Carrier Group during a critical period.

We installed facilities for furnishing light and power to airfields, using much Japanese equipment and material, and operated this system without a single break in service thought was necessary many times to make repairs to power lines during actual bombings. We built 47 miles of primary and secondary power lines; installed 10,000 feet of lighting, conduit, fixtures, etc., at one fighter strip; 12,000 feet of conduit and fixtures at another fighter strip; and 11,600 feet of wood conduit at another field. We maintained two power houses on a 24-hour basis. We operated the Tojo Ice Plant—built from Jap equipment—and produced 563,000 pounds of ice for the hospitals.

We handled 115,000 tons of freight from ships. To facilitate this handling, we built the Guadalcanal-Bougainville-Tokyo Railroad—6,443.5 lineal feet of railroad, including subgrade, bolting crossties to rail, installing sidings, switches, spurs, etc. During unloading operations four ships were bombed and casualties were suffered, but the crews remained at their posts and continued in the performance of their duty.

The logging crews cut and prepared 2300 piles and poles and supplied logs for 950,000 board feet of lumber sawed at the mill. For radio masts we supplied 42 special logs running up to 90 feet in length.

We installed 630,000 feet of wire for a communication system and operated this system at Tulagi. In this project we installed seven exchange trunk lines, 61 miles of underwater line, 12 miles of overhead wire, 230,000 feet of Army field wire, and 240,000 feet of submarine cable and fittings.

"In addition, this battalion completed 200-odd miscellaneous structures ranging from housing facilities to radio stations. Sections of the battalion manned guns at Tulagi and aboard ships, and our main body moved into its defense position on Guadalcanal during 'Condition Black.'

"Much of this work was performed during the rainy season and under unusually strenuous conditions of weather and combat. The battalion was consistently bombed, strafed, fired on by enemy artillery, and fired on by snipers.

"Our battalion experienced 184 alerts, totaling 206 hours and 40 minutes; was bombed 67 times; and sustained three hits in the camp area, one of which completely destroyed the galley. Eighteen members of the battalion were cited for courageous action, and the battalion received fourteen letters of commendation and sixteen letters of appreciation from commanding officers of Army and Marine units with which we have served.

"In spite of all precautionary measures possible under existing circumstances, conditions of weather, combat, supply and work assignments were such that 509 members of the battalion were infected with malaria and 427 have been evacuated for wounds and malaria.

"Regardless of these handicaps, the courage and morale of the battalion remained high, and on the last day of this tour of duty the 529 officers and men left of our original 956 were engaged on 11 projects, all of which were progressing satisfactorily."

It was at Guadalcanal that the Seabees came to be known as the "Can Do boys" of the service. The record of the 26th indicates how the appellation was won.

Mitsubishi A6M "Zero" fighter plane

4: The "Other Story" of Wake Island

SINCE THE SEABEES PERFORM SO VITAL and elementary a function in the war-making machinery, how can they be a new organization? Who filled the role of Seabees in all the past years and past wars before Pearl Harbor? How do they differ from the Army engineers? These are questions which invariably occur to the civilian when he is first confronted with this worldwide organization which was not even in existence on December 7, 1941.

To understand the answers requires some knowledge of the organization of the Navy, as well as some perception of the nature of this war. Too often when we think of the Navy we think only of ships or dive-bombers or Marines; yet a modern fleet without great, far-flung bases—without piers, drydocks, airdromes, vast storage and repair facilities—is like an automobile without filling stations. The mobility of both the air and surface elements of a fleet is directly related to the number and location of the bases. Moreover, as the character of naval warfare becomes more complex, as the components become larger, more varied, and more numerous, so must the bases become larger and more complex.

From the beginning of our naval history we have required construction and maintenance of shore facilities; but from the Revolution to Pearl Harbor, at yards both within the country and outside it, all work of any magnitude was done by civilian labor under private contract; the routine work was done by the civilian yard crews. At Brooklyn Navy Yard, at Mare Island or at Pearl Harbor, the men who built docks, warehouses, radio stations and hospitals—even the men who drydocked and repaired the ships— were civilians.

To plan its shore developments, to handle relations with private contractors, and to supervise the yard crews in maintenance and repair of the stations, the Navy had created its Civil Engineer Corps in 1842. Normally, thereafter, a few officers were chosen periodically for the CEC from the graduating class at the Naval Academy. The men chosen were sent to a first-rate engineering school—usually Rensselaer Polytechnic Institute—for a three-year course in civil engineering, and upon graduation they became officers of the CEC. As such, they were not command officers—command was reserved strictly for officers of the line—but staff officers, concerned with planning and contracting for whatever shore installations were authorized by Congress and ordered by the Secretary of the Navy.

Prior to 1892 we had no bases outside the continental limits of the United States. On their few adventures outside continental waters, our warships had utilized friendly ports and the coaling stations maintained for merchantmen. The British fleet was master of the seas; and since Britain was generally friendly, our own fleet had concerned itself with North America. In line with our foreign policy expressed in the Monroe Doctrine, our Navy was not an offensive weapon; it was our "first line of defense." In 1879, CEC officers surveyed a site at Pago Pago, Samoa, and in 1892 our first small but avowed foreign base was opened there.

With the Spanish War we extended our commitments from Puerto Rico to the Philippines. Unfortunately, we did not extend our naval establishment proportionately, but Congress did authorize a few foreign developments. Work was started at Pearl Harbor in 1901; at Puerto Rico in 1902; at Olangapo in the Philippines in 1902; at Guantanamo Bay, Cuba, in 1903. Dutch Harbor, Alaska, became a naval coaling station in 1902.

During the first World War there was some expansion of the shore Navy, but most of it was in the continental bases. Only $189,000,000 was spent by the Bureau of Yards & Docks for shore installations, and most of this went to expand the East Coast Navy yards. Much of the remainder went for aviation facilities, communication systems, and hospitals which CEC officers and civilian workers built in France, England and Ireland. After the war this construction reverted to our allies. Our Pacific positions received small attention: storage was increased at Guam, Pearl Harbor, Pago Pago and Cavite; and an ammunition depot was built at Olangapo. Considerable work was done at Coco Solo in the Canal Zone.

In retrospect, our naval enterprise in World War I was small potatoes. Except for the U-Boats, the Allied fleets held unchallenged control of the Atlantic. The airplane was a trivial factor in naval operations. The Pacific was as quiet as a millpond, and our warships and transports berthed in Europe at spacious, well-fitted docks which were never threatened by the enemy.

At the end of the last war the CEC, like all other branches of the Navy, felt the pinch of pacifism. During a period when we were scuttling our warships in a vain sacrificial gesture before the world, we certainly were not improving our shore establishments. By 1930 the CEC had only 126 officers to handle its entire planning and administrative program, from Puerto Rico to Olangapo. From 1918 to 1938—twenty fateful years in which Japan was rushing fortification of her mandated islands and the whole character of warfare was changing—development of our naval shore facilities was at a virtual standstill. A little work was started at Cavite and at Cold Bay, Alaska, in 1929; and some development of Johnston and Sand Islands, southwest of Hawaii, was begun in 1934. But for the most part the CEC marked time within its financial straitjacket.

No man in service was more restive under the restraint of pacifism than Vice Admiral Ben Moreell, present chief of Civil Engineers. Youngest vice admiral in the Navy and the first non-Annapolis man to attain such rank, he is as bellicose as any catskinner in the Seabees. A product of St. Louis and an honor graduate of Washington University, he joined the CEC in the first World War; then embarked on a twenty-year campaign to build up our defenses in the Pacific. "Let's get in or get out" became his *Carthago delenda est* and by 1928 he had become a special pleader for more emphasis on naval aviation.

In 1938, after Munich and after Japanese intentions in the Pacific had become obvious to many, our Government began to take the hobbles off the Navy. The CEC, still working through private contractors with civilian labor, began to expand fuel, flight and housing facilities at our overseas bases. The German march into Poland accelerated the process somewhat, but the fact remains that on June 22, 1940, when France fell, the United States Navy, ashore and afloat, was an antiquated, defensive organization incapable of making modern war at any distance from our own shores.

Puerto Rico was still our most advanced base in the Atlantic. In the Pacific, we had Pearl Harbor, and we can almost stop there. The tenuous line through Midway, Wake and Guam to Cavite was too long and too thin and too weak to be called a line of defense. Congress refused to authorize the fortification of Guam. The airfields in the Philippines were cow pastures.

The new American Navy dates from the destroyer deal with Britain. By that deal we began to build the two roads to victory in the Atlantic: the Argentina-Iceland-Londonderry road through the North Atlantic, and the Miami-Trinidad-Natal-Ascension-Freetown road through the South Atlantic.

Simultaneously, we began building three roads across the Pacific: the Sitka-Kodiak-Dutch Harbor-Adak-Attu road, the Pearl Harbor-Midway-Wake-Guam-Cavite road, and the Pearl Harbor-Palmyra-Canton-Samoa-Fiji-Espiritu Santo-Noumea road to Australia, the Solomons and the Indies.

In the final analysis this war, like most of history's wars, boils down to a fight for roads. The roads this time are the longest in history; indeed, they are as long as they can possibly be on a globe no larger than ours. Before America can bring her decisive industrial might to bear against her enemies, five roads must have been completed: the two roads to Germany, the three roads to Tokyo. These roads must be broad, because of the weight and variety of the weapons and supplies which must flow over them. They must be safe from successful attack.

The problem of Admiral Moreell and the Civil Engineer Corps in 1940 was to accelerate construction of these five roads. Varying amounts of work had been done on each road; but all five roads had to be converted into super-highways in the shortest possible time. The Army and our British allies would help; but the job was a Navy job.

Except for its incomparable magnitude, this road-building job had many of the aspects of the construction of the Union Pacific Railroad. The modern military roads had to be driven through steaming jungles, over ice-capped mountains, and through territory held by the enemy. The men building the roads would have to be prepared to throw aside their tools and pick up their rifles at the sound of a siren. Construction plans would have to be integrated with combat plans.

It is most interesting to note that as late as 1940, when the Bureau of Yards and Docks began in earnest the task of driving these roads to completion, we were still employing the system of private contract and civilian labor. We were using and proposed to continue using the private contractor and his civilian labor, not only to build our continental facilities, but also to build our most advanced bases. The organization of the Navy permitted no other system. The CEC officers were staff officers only; they could not command Navy personnel. It had been this way from the beginning; it would continue to be this way.

Swiftly and methodically, the CEC began negotiating cost-plus-fixed-fee contracts with combinations of private contractors. The contractors began their big push to recruit workmen for the overseas jobs. Attracted by the high wages, thousands of men embarked for Newfoundland, Iceland and the British Isles; for the West Indies; for Sitka, Kodiak and Dutch Harbor; for Pearl Harbor and the several nearby Hawaiian Islands; for Midway, Wake and Cavite; for Palmyra and Samoa.

Admiral Moreell and the Navy command watched the civilians embark with misgivings. Even in peacetime the use of civilians for advance base work has its handicaps. The men are not part of a military organization; they are not subject to military discipline. If a man for any reason doesn't want to work, he risks no more than loss of pay and job. Discontent, quite understandably, increases in proportion to the length of time away from home.

And what if suddenly we were drawn into the war?

The bombing plane has made this war different from all previous wars. Base construction is not only vulnerable to attack; it is the center of attack—the primary objective of the opposing forces.

The day after Christmas, 1940, twelve hundred civilians embarked from Pearl Harbor for Wake Island, led by red-headed, Irish Dan Teeters, 42-year-old construction engineer for Pacific Naval Air Bases, a contracting combine, these men were going to build an airfield, a sub base, a tank farm, gun emplacements, docks and housing on Wake. They were going to convert Wake into a strong section of the road to Tokyo. Families lined the pier as the ship sailed; the company had promised that the men would be back by Christmas Day, 1941.

What would happen to these men if the Japs attacked suddenly at Wake?

On December 6, 1941, approximately 70,000 civilians were working on projects outside the United States. They were building the two Atlantic and the three Pacific "roads."

At Argentia, Newfoundland, 5,158 persons were at work on the base, 1,809 of whom were Americans and the remainder natives.

In Iceland, 369 Americans and 105 Icelanders were building the Navy tank farm; the Army was doing the major work at this base.

At Londonderry, North Ireland, 5,664 persons were employed—1,167 Americans and 4,497 British and Irish.

In the West Indies: 6,420 were in the San Juan, Puerto Rico area; 1,560 were at Ensenada Honda, Puerto Rico; 1,725 were at Vieques, Puerto Rico; 1,887 were at St. Thomas, Virgin Islands; 466 were at Antigua and 1,048 at St. Lucia, British West Indies.

Other comparable numbers were at Trinidad, Jamaica, the Canal Zone and the Galapagos Islands. The majority of these were natives.

On the north Pacific road: 895 were at Sitka; 2,396 were at Kodiak; 1,076 were at Dutch Harbor. Virtually all of these were Americans.

On the central Pacific road: 7,000 were in the environs of Pearl Harbor; 1,931 were at Midway; 1,149 were at Wake; 71 were at Guam; 3,412 were at Cavite; 207 were working on the Melinta Tunnel on Corregidor. Except at Cavite most of these were Americans.

On the long road through the South Pacific—this road was scarcely begun—351 were at Palmyra; 462 were at Johnston; and 1,297 were at Samoa. All of these were Americans.

On December 6, these people were doing war work for a nation at peace with the world. But on December 7 their status had changed; they had become fair game for the bombs and shells of Germany, Italy and Japan. How did they react to the news from Pearl Harbor? Well, before we judge them too harshly, let's consider what happened to the men at Wake, Guam and Cavite. What happened to those men might have happened to all the rest.

The story of the men on Wake is told best by Mrs. Dan Teeters, the tall, blonde, affable wife of the superintendent. With her husband, she was aboard the ship which left Pearl Harbor on December 26, 1940. For eleven months, she was the only woman on Wake—with 350 Marines and 1,150 construction men. She left the island by Pan-American clipper on November 18, 1941, after being ordered out by the Navy because of the increasing danger.

"Dan had handpicked the men to go to Wake," Mrs. Teeters told me in Washington. "They were an extremely capable group of men. Some of them were young fellows still going to college. They had run out of money, so they were working a year on the island to save enough to finish their education. Others were older men who were laying up savings for their families and for their old age. When we arrived at Wake we built a temporary tent camp where we lived until the very nice permanent camp was completed. Later, the Marines came in and took over the tent camp. Dan and I had a cottage where we lived comfortably in spite of the heat.

"There was never any trouble about morale. It was a dry camp—no liquor and no women were allowed on the island. Dan had a three-cell jail built, but I was the only prisoner it ever had – some of the men locked me in as a joke one Sunday afternoon. We had no police, and the men just worked all the time and went to the movies at night. They were given one day off every two weeks. There are no mosquitoes at Wake—all the water is salt water—so the men wore shorts and sun helmets, and their bodies became the color of mahogany. They worked very hard, and we were far ahead of schedule on both the sub base and the air base.

"However, along in October and November you could feel the men becoming a little restless and uneasy. For one thing, they were nearing the end of their year. They wanted to go home, of course. Then, mysterious things were happening. Planes would drone over the island during the night, and no one would know whose planes they were. Dan and Jimmy Devereux (Major James P. S. Devereux, USMC, Chevy Chase, Md., commanding the Marine contingent) told the men that the planes were our planes using Wake as an objective in maneuvers. But the men didn't believe that story. No doubt it was the Japs coming up from the Marshalls. Ships would pass far offshore, and they would refuse to reply to radio requests for their identity. The men saw the ships; they knew that Wake was five hundred miles from any shipping lane; so, you couldn't blame them for being uneasy.

"The main reason for this uneasiness was that the men felt so exposed. Anticipating an attack isn't so bad if you have some protected place, like a forest, into which you can retreat and gather your strength. But out there on Wake the men were like frogs on a flat rock. Camouflage was ineffective. Everything was on top of the ground. The construction men were unarmed; if they attempted any resistance and were captured, they could be legally shot as guerrillas.

"The men regarded me as a sort of barometer. They figured that as long as I was allowed to stay on the island things couldn't be so bad. So, for this reason I used to take a walk nearly every afternoon, so the men could see me. Along in November the Navy began warning Dan that I'd have to leave, but I tried to stay because I knew that the men would become more uneasy when I left.

"Finally, Jimmy came over to the house and said that this time I would have to go. He had an order from Pearl Harbor for me to leave on the next plane; and you know that we don't argue when we hear that word 'order.' I left on the afternoon of November 18, and I'll never forget how some of the men looked when they saw me walking down to board the plane. I think that they realized then that they were In for it.

"I was in Honolulu when the attack came, and of course I was scared stiff for Dan and Jimmy and all the men. I hoped that the Navy could rescue them, and apparently Dan and Jimmy believed almost up to the last moment that a ship was coming in. Steve Bancroft, the Pan-Air pilot, brought me a letter from Dan on December 21. Dan told me that the first bomb had knocked our little house into a million pieces. He said that he was sitting in a dugout, and that almost everything had been destroyed, but that he felt sure that the Navy was coming in to take the men out. That was the last word I had until the Japs broadcast a recording of Dans voice: he reported that he was safe and in good health.

"Did Dan and the construction men fight the Japs? The movies insisted that they did, but they did not. Perhaps some of them helped pass ammunition up for the Marines, but, after all, the men had nothing to fight with. They could do little else but lie in their slit trenches while the Japs bombed and shelled them. When all the fuel and installations had been destroyed, and all hope of reinforcement had to be abandoned, then there was nothing else to do but surrender. When no help came, I think that both the Marines and the construction men felt that they had been let down.

"According to all the records that I have been able to gather since the surrender, 35 of the construction men were killed during the attack and 15 Marines. The Japs kept all the prisoners at Wake for about two weeks, then shipped them to prison camps at Shanghai. Instead of regarding the construction men as civilian internees, the Japs chose to regard them as prisoners of war.

When Dan and the men reached Shanghai, the Japs wanted to parade them through the streets; but Dan raised so much hell about it that they dropped the idea. That Dan really beats those Japs down; I imagine they'll be glad to be rid of him when the war is over. He appealed to the Germans and Italians in Shanghai to help him prevent the parade, and the Germans helped, since they weren't too happy about all the anti-white man jubilation.

"The Japs reported the names of 850 of the men within a few months after their capture. Then, almost two years later, they reported 205 more. The deaths of 35 have been verified; about 70 are still unreported. We—the contractors, the families of the men, the Navy, and the State Department—have made every effort to get the Japs to repatriate the construction men, but apparently there is little hope. The Japs insist that they are prisoners of war.

"We have no reason to think that the men have not received fairly decent treatment. The Red Cross has been able to deliver a number of package shipments, and the neutral reports that have trickled through say that there is a general lack of medicines and sufficiently warm clothing, but there have been no atrocities such as those reported in the Philippines.

"In March 1943, Dan, along with several British and American officers, escaped from the Woosung prison, but they ran into too much hard luck. A heavy fog came in, so they hid in a barn for several hours waiting for the fog to lift. A Chinese farmer betrayed them to the Japs, and they were recaptured. Dan was tried before a civil court and sentenced to ten years imprisonment. He is now at Ward Row Gaol in Shanghai. He's terribly impatient, of course, but a dentist who has been repatriated assured me that when he fixed Dan's teeth at the jail he seemed to be in good health.

Mrs. Teeters, whose home is in Los Angeles, spends much of her time in Washington where she serves as an energetic advocate for the Pacific Naval Air Bases Benefit Association—a sort of business and social organization of the families of all the construction men who are Jap prisoners. At the outset, the contracting companies established a fund to help these families in their peculiar emergency. The families are kept informed of all efforts being made to repatriate and to help the men. Letters are pooled, and a printed digest of excerpts is mailed to all people concerned.

Even though the optimism in the letters may be suspect, the excerpts give a running account of construction men in prison. Here are a few excerpts arranged in categories:

ATTACK ON WAKE

"SIEGE WAS TERRIBLE–SON SHOT IN HEEL FIRST DAY OF BATTLE, SECOND DAY SHOT IN SHOULDER AND ABDOMEN, DIED EVENING OF SECOND DAY, AND WAS BURIED IN COMMON GRAVE ALONG WITH (CENSORED) OTHER CASUALTIES—LOST EYEGLASSES AND ALL PERSONAL EFFECTS AT WAKE—THE THREE OF US CAME THROUGH THE FRACAS WITHOUT A SCRATCH—I LOST EVERYTHING BUT MY SHOES ON THE ISLAND—THEY SURE TOOK US BY SURPRISE; I WAS JUST GOING TO BARRACKS TO WASH FOR LUNCH—WE WERE TAKEN INTO CUSTODY ON DECEMBER 23 AND KEPT THERE UNDER GUARD UNTIL JANUARY 12; THEN THEY BROUGHT US TO CHINA."

ARRIVED SHANGHAI

"TOOK US TWELVE DAYS FROM WAKE ON THE BOAT— WONDERFUL TRIP TO SHANGHAI—WE WERE IN BAD CONDITION WHEN WE LANDED, BUT I AM GAINING WEIGHT— ARRIVED CHINA JANUARY 24."

CLIMATE AND WEATHER

"UNCOMFORTABLE COMING FROM TROPICS TO SHANGHAI CLIMATE IN JANUARY—ALTHOUGH THE WINTER WAS COLD WE ALL CAME THROUGH IN VERY GOOD SHAPE—HAVE SURE SEEN A CHANGE IN WEATHER AFTER BEING IN THE TROPICS; SNOW AND SLEET DIDN'T GO VERY WELL WITH TENNIS SHOES AND SHORTS—COUNTRY IS NOW GREEN AND PRETTY—

WEATHER ABOUT THE SAME AS NEW YORK—WEATHER ABOUT THE SAME AS ASOTIN, WASH.—THE WEATHER HERE IS ABOUT LIKE FRESNO—THE SUNSHINE IS NOT UNLIKE THAT AT HOME, ONLY THE ALTITUDE IS MUCH LOWER THAN WYOMING—THE WEATHER IS MUCH LIKE VANCOUVER."

LOCATION OF CAMP

"HOPING TO GET TO SEE SHANGHAI, BUT ALL I HAVE SEEN IS THE TOWERS FROM A DISTANCE—WE CAN SEE CHINESE OF ALL AGES WORKING IN THE FIELDS—WE ARE LIVING IN A VERY FERTILE, BEAUTIFUL COUNTRY—OUR CAMP COVERS ABOUT TWENTY-FIVE ACRES—OUR INTERNMENT CAMP WAS FORMERLY A JAPANESE CAVALRY CAMP.

BARRACKS

"OUR LIVING QUARTERS ARE GOOD BUILDINGS—WE LIVE IN WOODEN BARRACKS—WE ARE LIVING IN A LARGE MILITARY BARRACKS—WE HAVE MATERIALS TO MAKE THE CAMP COMFORTABLE—SCREENS AND MOSQUITO NETTING—WE HAVE GARDEN SEED AND FLOWERS."

CAMP GOVERNMENT

"I AM IN CHARGE OF THIRTY-SEVEN MEN, WHICH KEEPS ME BUSY—I AM A MESS SERGEANT FOR THE BARRACKS—THERE IS A LEADER FOR EACH BARRACKS AND WE HAVE TO LOOK AFTER THE WELFARE AND CONDUCT OF THE MEN—I AM IN CHARGE OF THIRTY-EIGHT MEN."

RECREATION

"CONFINED WITHIN A LIMITED SPACE, WE DO HAVE A FEW PLEASURES— BASEBALL AND VOLLEYBALL POPULAR IN THE EVENING—JAPANESE MILITARY BAND OCCASIONALLY—I FORMED A GLEE CLUB AND WE GIVE CONCERTS IN THE BARRACKS—PLAYING QUITE A BIT OF BRIDGE—THE JAPANESE HAVE GIVEN US TWO BAND CONCERTS WITH JAPANESE AND AMERICAN MUSIC— TEN CIGARETTES (CHINESE) 2 OR 3 TIMES A WEEK.

WORK

"CAMP BEING RECONSTRUCTED AND INTERNEES ARE IN CHARGE OF WORK—BUILDING BASEBALL FIELD—BIG GARDEN AND RAISING VARIETY OF VEGETABLES—PLANTING

EIGHT ACRES OF VEGETABLES FOR OUR OWN
CONSUMPTION—WE HAVE A LITTLE FARMING TO DO AND
BELIEVE ME WE HAVE A HELLUVA TIME GETTING SOME OF
THESE LAZY MEN OUT FOR THAT—DAD AND I HAVE BEEN
DOING CARPENTER WORK FOR THE LAST TWO MONTHS—WE
WORK SIX DAYS A WEEK—I KEEP BUSY REPAIRING
EYEGLASSES—I SPEND ALL SPARE TIME REPAIRING
WATCHES—I'M RAISING CHICKENS FOR THE JAPANESE—THE
JAPANESE HAVE STARTED A CHICKEN FARM AND PUT ME IN
CHARGE OF IT; I NOW HAVE 300 HENS—MY WORK IS
ELECTRICAL; I AM ONE OF THE FEW ELECTRICIANS IN CAMP—I
HAVE TAILORED A NEW SUMMER UNIFORM FOR A JAPANESE
BOY HERE IN CAMP—I'VE JUST UPHOLSTERED THE
FURNITURE FOR THE JAPANESE CAMP DIRECTOR—WE WORK
ON OUR VEGETABLE GARDEN JUST OUTSIDE THE ELECTRIC
FENCE—OUR TOMATOES, ONIONS, BEANS AND CABBAGE ARE
LOOKING NICE—THE MEN FIFTY AND OVER KEEP THE
BARRACKS CLEAN.

FOOD

"LOTS TO EAT—SIMPLE BUT SUFFICIENT—RICE AND STEW
TWICE AND BREAD AND STEW ONCE—I SURE HAVE LEARNED
TO LIKE RICE, HA! HA!—WE ARE GETTING AMPLE FOOD, AND
ARE BEING FED THREE TIMES A DAY; WE GET BREAD ONCE A
DAY, AND WITH THIS WE GET TEA AND SOMETIMES COFFEE
AND SUGAR—FOOD NOTHING EXTRA BUT SUFFICIENT—HOW
I DREAM OF MOTHER'S COOKING—TEA ALL THREE MEALS—I
HELP COOK FOR THE REST OF THE BOYS—WE HAVE HAD
COFFEE THREE OR FOUR TIMES, WHICH IS A TREAT—ON
EMPEROR'S BIRTHDAY ALL WERE GIVEN, PER MAN, ONE-HALF
POUND OF MARGARINE, TWO APPLES AND TWENTY
CIGARETTES; LONG LIVE THE SON OF HEAVEN!"

MEDICAL CARE

"OUR DOCTORS WORK WITH JAPANESE CAMP PHYSICIANS—
WE HAVE A HOSPITAL, THREE AMERICAN DOCTORS AND ONE
EXCELLENT JAPANESE ARMY DOCTOR—THE JAPANESE
DOCTOR AND OUR DOCTOR LOOK AFTER US—HAVE MEDICAL
ATTENTION AND ARE UNDER OUR OWN MARINE DOCTOR'S
CARE—A FAIRLY DECENT HOSPITAL AND TWO MARINE
DOCTORS AND ONE JAPANESE DOCTOR—THE JAPANESE
FURNISH US WITH TOOTHPASTE AND BRUSHES—MEDICAL

FACILITIES MUCH IMPROVED—ALL OUR WATER IS BOILED
BEFORE WE DRINK IT."

STUDIES

"I'M STUDYING SPANISH—IN EVENING, CLASSES ARE HELD IN
HISTORY, MATH AND SEVERAL LANGUAGES—I'M STUDYING
THE JAPANESE LANGUAGE—WE ARE STUDYING CHINESE AT
PRESENT BUT NOT MAKING MUCH PROGRESS; PRETTY
TOUGH—WE HAVE A CLASS IN PLUMBING—I'M TEACHING
BODYBUILDING TO A BUNCH OF ENGLISH, WAKE AND
TIENTSIN MARINES."

RELIGIONS

"PERMITTED TO HOLD CHURCH SERVICES–MOTHER MARY IS
WITH ME EVERY HOUR—I'M PRAYING EVERY DAY—I SAY THE
ROSARY EVERY MORNING AND PRAYERS EVERY NIGHT—THE
JAPANESE HAVE LET US KEEP OUR BIBLES AND HAVE
CHURCH."

CLOTHING

"THE JAPANESE ARMY HAS FURNISHED US UNIFORMS TO
WEAR—THE JAPANESE ISSUED US CLOTHES, SHOES AND
PERSONAL EQUIPMENT—WE WERE GIVEN BLANKETS ON OUR
ARRIVAL; LATER WE GOT WARM CLOTHING."

REQUESTS

"SEND ALL BULL DURHAM YOU CAN—SURE WOULD LIKE
SOME COPENHAGEN—SEND SOME KODAK PICTURES—SEND
ME TWO ROLLS OF COTTON AND FEEN-A-MINT—SEND SOME
SALT; SALT IS SCARCER IN CHINA THAN GOLD—SMOKING
TOBACCO AND CIGARETTE PAPERS WANTED—SEND A COUPLE
OF CARTONS OF BULL DURHAM—SMOKING PROBLEM IS
FIERCE—SEND ME FIVE BUCKS; I CAN USE IT IN THE
CANTEEN—SEND ME SOME PEANUT BRITTLE; I'M DYING FOR
SOME."

GENERAL

"PLEASE EXCUSE ME FOR NOT WRITING—WOULD HAVE
WRITTEN SOONER BUT SOMETHING HAS INTERFERED WITH
THE BOAT SCHEDULE—WE HAD FRENCH TOAST THIS
MORNING WITH PHEASANT EGGS, LOTS OF SALT—I HADN'T

EXPECTED TO COME TO CHINA, BUT WHEN THE OPPORTUNITY
PRESENTED ITSELF SO PERSISTENTLY I JUST COULDN'T
RESIST—READY TO SETTLE DOWN AND STOP ROAMING—IT
FEELS LIKE PLAYING ON THE WRONG TEAM, BUT WAIT UNTIL
THE NINTH INNING—I AM VISITING THE ORIENT WITH ALL
EXPENSES PAID—ALL I HAVE IS THE BIBLE GRANDDAD GAVE
ME AND THE BOOK, HOW TO WIN FRIENDS—I HOPE THE WAR
WON'T LAST AS LONG AS I THINK IT WILL—MOM, I DREAM OF
THOSE CHOCOLATE AND BUTTERSCOTCH PIES; ALSO OF
DOROTHY LAMOUR."

The seventy-one construction men at Guam, which was not fortified, were taken into Jap custody with only one tragic incident. One man, John Kluegel, of Honolulu, apparently figuring the forces had given up, rushed nervously out to surrender. A Jap soldier, also nervous, promptly bayoneted Kluegel to death. The rest were taken to Kobe, Japan, where all reports indicate they have had all the necessities and a few comforts.

Even now little is known of the fate of the 3,619 civilian workers at Cavite and Corregidor. Only a small percentage of these were Americans from the States; most of them were Filipinos and white men who were permanent residents of the islands. Presumably, the Filipinos were not interned, and the white men were taken to Santo Tomas, a name which connotes abuse and atrocity.

Of the CEC officers at Cavite three escaped. Lieutenant Daniel R. Dorsey (CEC, USNR, Wilmington, Del.) supervised the destruction of the tank farm and all oil installations on Mindanao before making a dramatic escape by fishing boat. Captain James D. Wilson (CEC, USN, Buntyn, Tenn.), in charge of all engineering, and Lieutenant Lewis G. Phillips (CEC, USNR, Washington, D.C.) also escaped, but the rest of the officers were taken prisoner. These include Lieutenant James R. Davis (CEC, USN, Altadena, Cal.); Lieutenant Cecil J. Espy (CEC, USN, Bonners Ferry, Idaho); Lieutenant Benjamin D. Goodier (CEC, USNR, Denver, Col.); Lieutenant George H. Greenwood (CEC, USNR, Stockton, Cal.); Lieutenant Commander Charles B. Snead (CEC, USNR, Sausalito, Cal.); Lieutenant Commander Jerry A. Steward (CEC, USNR, Streetman, Tex.); and Ensign William R. Yankey (CEC, USNR, Springfield, Ky.).

Three CEC officers were captured at Guam: Lieutenant (jg) Jack W. Schwartz (CEC, USNR, Los Angeles, Cal.); Ensign Francis J. Carney (CEC, USNR, Newport, R.I.); and Ensign Frank Wolfsheimer (CEC, USNR, Washington, D.C).

Four officers were captured at Wake: Lieutenant Commander Elmer B. Greey (CEC, USNR, Princeton, N.J.); Lieutenant (jg) James B. Robinson (CEC, USNR, Rockville, Md.); Ensign Robert C. Walish (CEC, USNR, Milwaukee, Wis.); and Ensign Belmont N. Williams (CEC, USNR, Schenectady, N.Y.).

It is difficult to exaggerate the complexity of the legal and human problems which arose out of these hundreds of civilians being captured by the enemy and considered as prisoners of war. The men were employees of private contractors; as such, they were protected by workmen's compensation laws; but the Navy was under no legal responsibility either for their welfare or for their wages. Moreover, laws governing expenditures by the Navy expressly prohibited the Navy's paying the families of these men.

The contractors were in just as difficult a position. They were not obligated to continue paying the men, since the contract had been "breached by a third party." And even if the contractors were willing and able to continue payment, the cost-plus-fixed-fee Government contract made this difficult, if not impossible.

In this unprecedented emergency, Admiral Moreell stepped in and instructed the contractors to pay each family $100 for the month of January 1942. He then retained an insurance company to investigate the small army of dependents who had suddenly come to life and laid the matter before the President. Meantime, he authorized another $100 payment for February.

The President initiated action whereby the Government assumed responsibility for the men and their dependents. The Federal Security Administrator set up a schedule of benefits, and the sum of $5,000,000 was taken from one of the President's funds to pay these benefits. Payments were made under this plan up to January 1, 1943.

In December 1942, Congress passed an act whereby such men who are captured or missing in a war zone would be considered totally disabled and entitled to the equivalent of disability benefits under the Longshoreman's Act. In December 1943, benefit payments under the Longshoreman's Act were liberalized and increased. The men were to be treated as though they had been civil service employees; their families were to be paid 70 percent of the comparable civil service wage scale at Pearl Harbor, and the other 30 percent was to be held for the prisoners return. The maximum death benefit under this act is $7,500, but as long as the man remains alive and out of this country, full disability benefits will continue to be paid, even though the total far exceeds the $7,500.

One unreported employee's mother writes long, boiling letters each month criticizing the conduct of the war, offering suggestions as to strategy, and asking why-the-hell the Navy doesn't "threaten the Japs more fiercely."

A movement is underway, however, to properly award one prisoner's wife for her unexampled patience and philosophical attitude in time of war. Recently she addressed her first letter to the Navy Department.

"Sirs," she said: "Not having heard from my husband in two years, I am beginning to feel that he must be detained somewhere."

How did the civilian workers at bases which were not attacked by the enemy react to the news from Pearl Harbor? They reacted variously, as might be expected. Some of them gripped their tools harder, stuck to their jobs. At a few bases, many requested immediate transportation home. The general reaction confirmed what the CEC had long feared: the civilian-worker plan for advance bases was outmoded; it was not for this war.

In the darkest hours of our history, we were condemned to mark time while a whole new organization for overseas construction was built. Thousands of civilians had to be evacuated from strategic areas, and they had to be replaced by skilled construction men who were armed, trained and equipped members of a military unit.

The Jap attack caught us short in many categories. Our shortage of first-class warships and planes has been widely discussed and is generally understood. What needs explanation is that the Japs caught us not only short of bases; they also caught us without an organization with which to build bases!

Our war in the Pacific and, to a lesser extent, our war in the Atlantic had to mark time while we dismantled the private-contract-civilian-labor system for advance-base construction; while we enlisted construction men and built the Seabee organization;

and while we substituted Seabees for civilians. When you understand what this meant in time, shipping and expense, you will
understand why so many long, bitter months passed before an
offensive blow could be struck in the Pacific.

To substitute Seabees for civilians in the shortest possible
time was the task assumed by Admiral Moreell and the Civil Engineer Corps in December 1941.

African American Seabees

Battle of Peleliu, 1944.

5: The Seabees Are Born

SIX WEEKS BEFORE PEARL HARBOR, the civilian labor situation in Iceland had deteriorated to a point where something had to be done. It became impossible to persuade American workmen to stay there. Sky-high wages and bonuses were not enough. The weather was depressing, and the Icelanders were less than cordial. To meet this minor emergency Admiral Moreell obtained authorization for five companies of 99 men each (495 men) to be enlisted in the Navy for construction duty in Iceland. There was no place to train these men as a construction unit, so they began reporting to the regular Naval Training Station at Newport, R.I. But they never reached Iceland. The blow at Pearl Harbor wrecked the civilian-worker system in both oceans and brought such frantic demands from the Pacific that Iceland had to be forgotten.

There was an imperative call for 300 construction men to leave for the South Pacific at once! The Navy met this demand by taking 197 men who had been enlisted for duty in Iceland, adding 103 Navy general service recruits, and rushing them to a waiting convoy. Heavy equipment for these men was loaded on trucks at Quonset Point, R.I., and the police-escorted trucks raced for the waiting ships. So important was this expedition that the men were divided among ships in the convoy so that one sinking would not be too disastrous.

The destination? Bora Bora, a small island in the Society group about 140 miles from Tahiti. Remember, this was January 1942, a month after the attack at Pearl Harbor and long before the fall of either Singapore or Bataan. Why, then, were we rushing a construction expedition to a remote island that was 3,000 miles from MacArthur's men in the Philippines?

Here's the explanation. On the night of December 7, 1941, the assumption was that Japan would overrun the Philippines and the Indies. Our Navy, for lack of bases would have to fall back, back, and back, like a boxer trying to regain balance after a heavy, unexpected blow. Where the Navy would regain its balance would depend upon its bases. In the Central Pacific, Pearl Harbor might be counted upon to hold. But in the South Pacific we had only the thin line extending through Palmyra to Samoa. If we were to stop the Japs in the South Pacific, we had to select spots at which we could concentrate sufficient strength before the Japs overran them.

The Navy planners began to draw lines on maps. If you draw a straight line around the earth from the Panama Canal to the Coral Sea, the line will pass through the Society Islands. So, in December 1941, Bora Bora had been selected as the spot to build a tank farm to store the fuel that was to power the ships and the planes which were to fight the Battle of the Coral Sea. That's why the first construction detachment ever to wear the uniform of the United States Navy was being rushed to Bora Bora in the first weeks of 1942.

The men christened themselves "Bobcats." Most of the Navy general service contingent were youngsters with little skill or experience. They squawked loudly about having been shanghaied for construction work, though later some of them transferred to the Seabees. The construction volunteers, however, were older men, highly skilled, many of them veterans of the first World War. This convoy arrived at Bora Bora on February 17. There were no piers, so the Bobcats assembled a pontoon barge and began unloading seaplanes, defensive guns, and equipment for the tank farm. Rain fell steadily; food was strictly out of the can; the men suffered severely from dysentery, and some of them came down with elephantiasis; it was eight weeks before the first mail arrived from home. But the Bobcats stuck to the job. They emplaced heavy guns. They built a seaplane ramp. They installed and camouflaged the vast storage tanks, then filled the tanks from fat tankers. They cleared an airstrip for the Army. And when our ships gathered for the Battle of the Coral Sea, May 4-8, Bora Bora was ready.

Meanwhile, in December 1941, the Navy rushed its plans for a military construction organization. Organizational problems were multifold; training facilities had to be found and built; mountains of supplies and equipment had to be accumulated; and, above all, skilled men—the kind who could not be drafted— had to be recruited. On December 28 the Seabees were officially born when the first naval construction regiment (3,000 men) was authorized. New authorizations came faster than the men could be assembled: 10,000; 20,000; 50,000; 100,000; 250,000!

To iron out all organizational red tape, Admiral Moreell relied upon Captain John R. Perry (CEC, USN, Waco, Tex.), a tall, red-headed Texan who specializes in damning torpedoes and driving full-speed ahead. The first hitch developed over officers. To obtain officers, the CEC proposed simply to expand itself; to seek out construction engineers, commission them according to their civilian attainments, and put them in command of the Seabees. But command had always been the prerogative of line officers of the Navy. The CEC had never commanded; why should it now? Reluctantly, the Navy agreed to the innovation, and the CEC began commissioning civilian engineers for the Seabees in ranks up to lieutenant-commander.

The second organization snarl was over "rates" for Seabees. Navy system called for every man to enter the Navy as an apprentice seaman; for promotion to come only after he had proved himself in uniform. Normally, this is an excellent plan, but the times were abnormal. Men wanted for the Seabees were skilled, experienced men; most of them had families; the draft wouldn't reach them for years. They would volunteer, but only if they had support for their wives and children.

Captain Perry asked the Bureau of Naval Personnel for permission to enlist men for the Seabees in rates up to and including chief petty officer. This would mean a sliding-scale of pay and allowances for Seabees from $50 to more than $200 a month. Naturally, the "regular" Navy men; men who had worked in the Navy for sixteen years to become chief petty officers—would resent thousands of newly created Seabee rates. Captain Perry pointed out, however, that the Navy recognized civilian attainment in commissioning officers, and he contended that this same practice should prevail in enlisting men.

These two major concessions by the Navy—the granting of command to CEC officers and the approval for rates-on-enlistment for men—made the Seabee organization possible. The CEC expanded itself from the 126 officers of the '30's to more than 8,000 officers, most of whom are assigned to the Seabees. The men were enlisted at an average rate of petty officer second class—average pay and allowances $140 a month—making the Seabees one of the highest paid organizations in the service.

In short, the Navy made it possible for the cream of the construction industry to join the Navy en masse. The civilian engineers became officers; the foremen became chief petty officers; the carpenters, machinists, earth movers, etc., became rates in the ranks. The Navy did more than make an affiance with the construction industry; it simply absorbed a large portion of the industry with amazingly successful results.

In this process of absorption, the Navy enjoyed the cooperation of both management and the labor unions. The construction companies were asked to release all the engineers who could be spared, and most of them responded quickly. The labor unions moved more cautiously. The leaders of the powerful building trades unions were concerned over the possibility that a Seabee organization might be used for Navy construction within the country's continental limits. If the Navy built a construction organization of its own, would the Navy use its organization to break possible strikes on Navy projects within the country?

Repeatedly, some of the union leaders asked Admiral Moreell for a guarantee that Seabees would not be used on continental projects. The admiral refused to give such a guarantee. He did, however, assure the unions that the Seabee organization was being built primarily for advance base work; that the CEC expected to continue building all continental facilities by private contract and civilian labor. Unless unforeseen emergencies developed, the Secretary of the Navy told the unions, the Seabees would do only such work within the country as was connected with their training. On this assurance he asked the unions for their cooperation in the recruiting drives, and most of the unions lent their aid. The Building Trades Council of the American Federation of Labor was particularly helpful.

It is impossible to exaggerate the terrible urgency for Seabee battalions in the spring of 1942. In all other branches of the service, we at least had a vestigial organization. But the Seabees—the skilled men who had to help lead the way across the Pacific—had to be organized from scratch, trained, equipped and transported; and because they had to go first, our war had to wait upon them. Long before we were attacked we had begun training other outfits, but we waited until after we were attacked to begin organizing the outfit which had to clear the way.

Where were the Seabees to be trained? In the training crisis the National Youth Administration, headed by Aubrey Williams, came to the rescue and thereby earned the eternal gratitude of the Navy. The NYA had small camps scattered throughout the country, and it was at these camps that many of the Seabees were concentrated for their medical shots, outfitting and brief conditioning. The various NYA camps took men in groups of 200 to 300, and these groups were assembled into battalions at the advance base depots.

The Seabees were not really trained during the first months; they were just assembled, given their medical shots and equipped with whatever was at hand. There was no time for training. The First and Second Battalions embarked from the West Coast for the South Pacific early in February 1942. The Third Battalion went to the Fijis; the Fourth to Dutch Harbor; the Fifth to Samoa. The Seabees had No.1 priority on shipping—volunteer firemen being rushed to the fire. Twenty-five battalions had been shipped overseas before the CEC could stabilize on an eight-week assembly and training period! There were desperate shortages of ordnance, construction equipment and clothing, so the battalions had to be shipped out with "supplies and equipment to follow." On arrival at their jungle islands, the men had to barter, steal and improvise while they waited and hoped for all the stuff that was "to follow."

On January 17, 1942, ground was broken near Norfolk for Camp Allen, which was to take care of one regiment. This camp was put in commission on March 13, when 2,000 men arrived there for training. Captain John G. Ware, USN, (Ret.) was the commanding officer, and the late Captain Harry A. Bolles (CEC, USN, Seattle, Wash.) was executive officer. The NYA camps, however, continued to be used until May 1942, when Camp Bradford was opened. Camp Bradford was ten miles from Camp Allen, but the two were operated as one training center.

It took months to lick the training problem. Camp Endicott, R.I., with a capacity of 11,000 men, was commissioned August 11, 1942; and Camp Peary, Va., with a capacity of 40,000 men, was opened in November 1942. These were followed by the commissioning of Camp Lee-Stephenson, Quoddy Village, Me.; the opening of the Recuperation Center at Camp Parks, Cal.; and the development of the Advance Base Depots at Port Hueneme, Cal.; Davisville, R.I.; and Gulfport, Miss.

In the fall of 1942, about the time that the creation of the construction battalions slowed down to an orderly process, the

Navy ordered the CEC to begin creating stevedore battalions of Seabees. A serious bottleneck had developed in the South Pacific. Ships could not be unloaded as fast as they arrived, and at one time eighty-three freighters were riding at anchor in the South Pacific waiting to be unloaded. Unloading difficulties were multiplied by the fact that we had no cargo docks north of Australia, and all cargo had to be handled first onto lighters, from the lighters to trucks, and thence to storage areas.

Also, it seems fair to say that civilian merchant seamen were no more enthusiastic about working under bombs than civilian construction crews had been. Much was said at home about merchant crews refusing to unload cargo at Guadalcanal. Perhaps these charges were too severe, but it was found that Seabees—even Seabees from the construction battalions—could unload a ship faster than as civilian crews. If Seabees with no stevedore experience could do so well, then why not enlist and train Seabees as stevedores and form them into stevedore battalions?

These stevedore battalions were designated as "Special" Seabee battalions, and the First Special was organized hastily and sent to Guadalcanal. Each Special battalion was organized around the nucleus of experienced stevedores, and the inexperienced men were given brief training on a dry-land model of a Liberty ship at Camp Peary. Thirty stevedore battalions have been organized.

A later development was the Construction Battalion Maintenance Unit. These units vary in size from 60 to 250 officers and men and are designed to replace construction battalions after construction has been completed and the war has moved on, leaving only maintenance and operations tasks in its wake. For instance, at Guadalcanal or Sitka or Iceland there is now no need for full construction battalions. The installations have been built; the war has moved on; so, Seabee maintenance units are keeping the lights burning and the fuel flowing from tankers to tank farms to bombing planes.

By 1943, with the pressure slacking off in both the Atlantic and the Pacific, the training period for Seabee battalions was gradually lengthened to three months. Battalions returning from overseas were given the military training which they skipped in the dark days. The Seabees began looking like a military organization as well as acting like one. On broad training grounds at the big camps, Marine Corps instructors taught the Seabees all the tricks of beach landings and jungle warfare. Tough bulldozer operators to whom fighting is an occupational sport were taught judo and bayonet tactics.

Remnants of a Mitsubishi A6M3 crash

Munda Airfield, Central Solomons, 1943

6: Between Pearl Harbor and Guadalcanal

THUS FAR I HAVE DETAILED THE evolution of the Seabees; I have told of their role in the drama at Guadalcanal; I have described the construction battle for Munda which was our first push north from Guadalcanal. In subsequent chapters I shall tell of Seabee adventures in the rest of the world; then I shall return to the Pacific to discuss the drives that "built the ring around Rabaul." Here, however, I want to go back to the summer of 1942 and relate how Seabee efforts in the South Pacific helped to make possible our landing at Guadalcanal.

No one can tell this story better than Sam Mathis (Lieutenant Commander Samuel J. Mathis, CEC, USNR, Blackville, S.C.), a youthful, soft-voiced engineering dynamo who had as big a part in stopping the Japs as any man in an American uniform. On May 4, 1942, the day on which the Japs landed at Guadalcanal and the day on which the Battle of the Coral Sea began, Mathis landed with a detachment of the First Seabee Battalion at Efate in the New Hebrides Islands.

"It was a picture-book May morning when we reached the harbor at Vila," Mathis related. "The blue water, green foliage and red-topped buildings reminded you of a technicolor movie. The Army had moved into New Caledonia 300 miles to the south; the Japs were moving into Guadalcanal 700 miles to the north; and we were moving into the New Hebrides to try to open up airstrips from which we could start bombing the Japs.

"The war down there was just a race between the Japs and the Americans. If the Japs could put Henderson Field into operation before we could start bombing them from the New Hebrides, then the Japs would run us out. If we got our planes over Henderson Field before the Japs could complete it, then maybe we could pave the way for a landing.

"I went ashore with Lieutenant Harry N. Wallin, Jr. (CEC, USN, Seattle, Wash.), who was our officer in charge, and we met Colonel Fassit of the Fourth Defense Marines, a detachment of which had landed on Efate a few days before. There was also a Marine aviation squadron there commanded by Joe Bauer (Lieutenant Colonel Harold W. Bauer, Coronado, Cal.), but the squadron didn't have any planes. There were a few Army Engineers under Lieutenant Elliott, and our problem was to scrape up enough equipment among us to build an airfield.

"The Marines and Engineers had cleared about 1,500 feet of runway, and they were damn glad to see the Seabees coming. We moved 506 officers and men ashore, took charge of the airstrip and began setting up our camp. But our equipment was still very meager, even after we had pooled resources with the Army and Marines. Our total construction equipment included one crane, ten trucks, two motor patrol graders, one pull-type grader, one D-8 bulldozer, two HD-14 bulldozers, four little D-4 'dozers, and one Gallion scarifier. One of the graders belonged to the Army, two of the bulldozers belonged to the Marines, and the rest was Seabee stuff.

"It was funny to look out there on that field and see them working. We had natives, soldiers, Marines, Marine pilots and Seabees all working together. The Seabees were running the machines, and the rest of them were doing the unskilled work. The big job was to keep that equipment from breaking down. Chief Farnham (Orville L. Farnham, Chief Carpenter's Mate, Jennings Lodge, Ore.) was in charge of our maintenance, and he was an old-time Irish construction man who knew every bolt and screw by its first name. He really kept that job going.

"May 28 was our first red letter day. On that day twenty planes arrived for Joe Bauer's squadron, and we opened up the first strip. Nothing makes men feel so good as when those first planes go into the air. It's just like opening an umbrella when you get caught in a drizzling rain.

"Meantime, the detachment had some other projects underway. We had to open up a seaplane base, so a squadron of PBY's could start bombing Guadalcanal. We had walked all over that blamed island and had selected a spot about seventeen miles from Vila for the seaplane base. This spot was called Havannah Harbor. There wasn't any road to the place, but we could make the seventeen miles in a day by pushing a jeep. That's how rough it was. Lieutenant Thomas J. Redican (CEC, USNR, Freeport, Ill.) took a detachment of men and moved over there and started building the base. They built a ramp out of wire mesh, and it's a good thing they had that ramp ready, because the first PBY to come in there hit a coral head and busted her bottom clear out.

"We had to get gasoline and bombs over to Havannah Harbor for the PBY's, so we'd hook a tractor up to a bunch of bomb trailers and start out. Usually it took about three days for the tractor to make the trip. But on June 1, those PBT's started dropping bombs on the Japs at Guadalcanal.

"Colonel Stevenson (USMC) and I walked all over the island looking for gun emplacement sites and for another airfield site. The whole island was mountainous jungle, but there was one spot up on the north side that was the most perfect site for an airfield I ever saw: I couldn't believe it when I first saw it. It was a spot about the size of a bomber strip right in the middle of jungle, yet there was no jungle on it. It was an area of hot Sulphur springs, and somehow the trees wouldn't grow on it. We converted it into a bomber strip with comparatively no effort at all. Nature was against us most of the time, but she sure played on our team there.

"Another project that we were rushing just as fast as the airstrips was a base hospital. This may seem strange to civilians, but we couldn't start a land offensive against the Japs until we had the hospital ready. Bill Clampet (Lieutenant Wm. T. Clampet, CEC, USNR, Brooklyn, N.Y.) and his detachment built the hospital. It had a 600-bed capacity, but at one time it had more than 900 patients. The Seabees who built that hospital were really proud of their work, and they had a right to be. Chief Carpenter's Mate George O. Bookout (Norfolk, Va.) and Chief Carpenter's Mate Liston L. Mallard (Kingston, N.C.) were in charge of the construction; Chief Electrician's Mate Harold L. Chapman (Claremont, N.H.) put in the plumbing; and Chief Electrician's Mate William D. Scott (Macon, Ga.) installed all the electrical appliances. That work went on twenty-four hours a day; the men suffered some from dysentery; but they felt rewarded when they saw those wounded Marines streaming into the hospital from Guadalcanal.

"All through June the PBY's kept bombing Guadalcanal from Havannah Harbor, but it was a 1,400-mile round trip, and we knew we were going to have to have an airfield closer to Guadalcanal before we could bomb the Japs effectively. So, on June 28, the base skipper, myself and a British Intelligence officer named Josslyn set out to explore the islands north of Efate in an effort to find an airfield site as close as possible to Guadalcanal. We flew up to Espiritu Santo, the northernmost tip of the New Hebrides, then we took a native fishing boat and went up as far as Santa Cruz inspecting islands. We went ashore on several islands, talked to a few natives, but we could find no possible airfield sites. Those islands are nothing but mountains sticking up out of the water and covered with jungle.

"Finally, we gave up and came on back to Espiritu Santo. It's about 200 miles north of Efate and about 500 miles from Henderson Field. We had wanted to get closer to Henderson Field, but it was impossible, so we selected a site at Espiritu Santo. Admiral McCain (Vice Admiral John S. McCain, USN, Carrollton, Miss.) came up and told us the field at Espiritu Santo had to be ready on July 28.

"Joe Bauer and I laid out the airstrip. Then we went back to Vila and started loading that night. We put the equipment on the ship, and Wallin selected thirty-five Seabee equipment operators to go along. We had one Marine AA battery to protect us, and a company of colored Army infantry to do the unskilled work.

"We arrived at Espiritu Santo on the afternoon of July 8. There wasn't a damn thing there but jungle. We began unloading and clearing. When we had unloaded our ship, it went back for a load of gasoline and bombs. We set up floodlights and worked around the clock. I had twelve Seabees who operated nine big pieces of equipment twenty-four hours a day for a month. You can figure out for yourself how much sleep they got. On a typical day—say July 21—here is who we had working on the field: 295 Army infantrymen, 90 Marines, 32 Seabees and 50 natives. The Seabees were running the equipment; the rest were clearing by hand. We had six tractors, two scrapers, one grease truck, one gas-wagon, three weapons carriers and one 50-kw. light generator. That's every last man and piece of equipment we had at Espiritu Santo—just 500 miles from the Japs.

"We cleared and surfaced 6,000 feet of runway, but we didn't cover the runway with Marston mat. We didn't have any mat. We just graded and rolled the coral. On July 28 we made our deadline. The first squadron of fighters came in. Then on July 29 the big boys came in—one squadron of B-17's. We fueled them from drums, and on July 30 they gave the Japs the first big pasting. We had to work around the clock right on, getting the fuel supply lines set up. In fact, during the next seven days we did little else than lug bombs and gasoline.

"By August second or third it seemed as if the whole Air Force and Marine Corps was pouring into our camp. Our little thirty-five-man galley went on a twenty-four-hour schedule of its own, feeding those air squadrons. On August 7, the Marines began landing at Henderson Field, and our field at Espiritu Santo became the vital link between our fields at Noumea and Efate and Henderson Field. The men who did this work deserve a lot of credit from the folks back home. You didn't see their pictures in the newspapers, because there was nothing glamorous or exciting about what they did. But I watched them work, and I have never felt such cold determination among a group of men. You felt that there was nothing in God's world they couldn't do if they decided to do it.

"I can't say too much for Chief Farnham. He went with me to Espiritu Santo, and it was he who kept the machinery rolling. Buckwalter (Melvin C. Buckwalter, Chief Carpenter's Mate, Laurens, Iowa), Prescott (Jack A. Prescott, Chief Shipfitter, Grand Meadows, Minn.), McCarthy (Harold C. McCarthy, Chief Machinist's Mate, Mason City, Wash.), and the Kreger brothers (Paul, Chief Machinist's Mate, and Fred, First Class Machinist's Mate, of Portland, Ore.) were all the kind of construction men who know how to do everything but quit. When you have men like them on your side, you feel you can't lose.

"Chief William K. Owens, Sr. (Chief Carpenter's Mate, Springfield, Ill.), was an old chap, past fifty, who had eight children. But he was an old-school construction man. He had charge of building storehouses, so to save his time he camped in the woods near his work. He must have averaged eighteen hours a day for weeks.

"Chief Nathan Hopper (Chief Shipfitter, Coal Bluff, Ind.) at the tank farm; Chief Charles W. Compton (Chief Carpenter's Mate, Latrobe, Pa.) at the waterfront; Chief Joseph A. Giovanni (Chief Carpenter's Mate, Jeanette, Pa.), who built the housing near the hospital; Chief Ben O. Gibbs (Chief Storekeeper, Webster Grove, Mo.), who handled our storage area—all of these men worked tirelessly and heroically to do the job.

"No man has more admiration for the courage of American flyers than I: the day Joe Bauer was shot down was the darkest day of the war for me. But when I think of American courage and guts, I'll always remember that sandy-haired Irishman, Chief Farnham, and how he kept those tractors and graders rolling night and day so that we could meet the deadline for the bombers going to Guadalcanal.

"And in case the Marine correspondents overlook him, I want to pay my respects to one more man. He was an old sergeant major named Woolley. He flew a Marine seaplane by the seat of his pants. He knew little about navigation, but he could fly anywhere and always came back. At Efate and Espiritu Santo, we had no spare parts for our machines. So, Woolley would fly down to Noumea, get a planeload of parts from the Army and Marines down there, and bring them back to us.

"But his most amazing performance was when he rescued one of our boys from a lonely island. When we went on the exploring trip up in the Santa Cruz Islands, we left four or five boys up in there to do some further exploring. I also had gone ashore at one uninhabited spot, and, completely by chance, I had left a drum of gasoline somewhere on that jungle island. Well, several weeks after the trip, we got word from one of those boys that he was sick with blackwater fever. How the hell were we going to reach him quickly?

"We called Woolley and told him the story. We described approximately how the island looked where the sick boy was. Woolley took off. Somehow—God knows how—he found the island and the sick boy. But that's only the beginning. He ran out of gas up there, and, believe it or not, without even knowing that we had left the gasoline drum up there, he found that gasoline and came back safe. And I'll swear that the sick man and the gas drum were not even on the same island!"

Before the South Pacific war could move northward from Guadalcanal in 1943, many Seabee battalions had labored to make the "road" strong and safe from Pearl Harbor to the Solomons. Detachments of the Fifth and 76th Battalions worked at Palmyra; detachments of the Fifth and 10th worked at Johnston and Canton Islands. In the Samoan Islands, we built a whole new world. The Second Battalion began work at both British and American Samoa only a few days after the First Battalion had landed at Efate. In both the Fiji and Ellice groups, vast construction projects were completed. A detachment of the Third Battalion developed Nandi in the Fijis, while the 58th and another detachment of the Third developed Vunda Point. Funafuti in the Ellice group was converted into a base by detachments of the First and Third; Nanomea was developed by the 16th; Nukupe-tauby another detachment of the 16th; Upolu by a detachment of the Second. Noumea, the great base in New Caledonia, was created by the 78th, 53rd, 19th, 11th and 20th Battalions.

The Sixth and Seventh Battalions arrived at Espiritu Santo in August 1942. The Sixth, of course, proceeded at once to Guadalcanal, where it fought the battle of Henderson Field; while the Seventh remained at Espiritu Santo to continue the work begun by Commander Mathis' sturdy pioneers. The 36th, 40th, 44th and 57th Battalions later poured into Espiritu Santo to expand it into a powerful base.

Each of these battalions has its own variation of the jungle island story. All of them were disappointed at not meeting the Japs; all of them continue to hope that their next assignment will be up where the bombs are falling. Every Seabee among them sorrowfully reported that he found nothing remotely resembling Dorothy Lamour; that drinking whiskey was painfully scarce; and that he preferred sawdust to another helping of Spam.

Virtually every one of these battalions had to unload its equipment onto pontoon barges, then drive the barges into strange beaches. Camps had to be cleared; weather had to be fought; disease had to be accepted with fortitude. Long waits for mail were the rule, not the exception. Yet morale continued wonderfully high among the men because (1) they were older construction men, accustomed to making homes for themselves under difficult, lonely conditions; and (2) they had volunteered to do a job on which they expected hardship.

A letter from Irvin E. Olson (Chief Carpenter's Mate, 60th Battalion, Waukegan, Ill.), written from Woodlark Island, illustrates a common experience and attitude:

"Our home is a tent on an island in the South Pacific. It is a coral island with about 6 to 12 inches of clay covering the coral, and there is dense jungle growth. There are coral reefs out around the island which protrude a bit above the water, also some which are submerged, making it dangerous for boats. There are high cliffs and beautiful beaches that have the finest, softest white sand. The water is just perfect for swimming, and we certainly do take advantage of that—almost every morning about six o'clock. There are hundreds of coconut palms, as before the war they were cultivated by a plantation owner who had imported some natives from Java to do the work. But on our arrival the island was in a sad state of affairs. Some of the natives still live on the island, and the males are giving us a hand in clearing the underbrush.

"These natives are not Negroes, but of a dark, honey-brown color, and have long, bushy hair in which some of them wear bamboo combs. They are very small people, but they can do heavy work. It is surprising how they shoulder heavy logs and, too, they stay right at it all day long, every now and then singing songs and giving out queer-sounding yells. They eat coconuts, roots, and a sort of wild cabbage, which they wash down with green coconut juice. Their teeth are coal black, that is, those who have teeth. They are very friendly and cooperative.

"We are living in regular army tents pitched in the jungles. Most of the fellows live back in the tall trees, but a few live here and a few there—just any place that is halfway cleared and close to the work. An entirely new camp is now being built—tents with wood floors up off the ground a few feet to keep out the dampness. When the camp is completed I am sure it will be a lot drier and a lot further away from the ants and lizards. As I have been writing this, my two tent mates, Jump (Chief Carpenter's Mate Hayes O. Jump, Glendale, Ky.) and Huff (Chief Carpenter's Mate Harley W. Huff, Cedar Rapids, Iowa) came in. Jump was slipping into his house moccasins with his bare feet and let out a blood-curdling yell. He had put his foot into a moccasin that a lizard was using for a bed. At the same time, while Huff and I were laughing, a big black bug, almost as big as a fruit-jar cap, started crawling over Huff's collar onto his neck, and he let out a yell and brushed it off onto Jump, who jumped through the side of the tent. Gosh, what a circus!

"At present we live in one of a group of ten tents, among which are a blacksmith shop, a machine shop and two tool tents. We sure have a swell bunch of fellows in our little village, about twenty in all. We call our town Betzville in honor of the only officer [Ensign Regis Joseph Beta, CEC, USNR, Allison Park, Pa.] who lives with us. Our little street is paved with coral, graded and rolled hard. We call it Jump's Boulevard. We also have an alley that we call Huff's Alley—it leads to the latrine. Quite a town, don't you think? Since we have the shops in our midst which need electric power and lights, we also have electric lights in our tents. Ritzy!

"The days are long, but there is always plenty of work to do. Lots of work day and night. Seabees at work! And they are the finest bunch of workers I've ever seen in one group. All trades and classes pulling in the same direction to complete our job in record time, and we really are breaking all previous records for the type of work we are doing. Our C.O. can well be proud of the 60th Battalion, and the 60th likes him. We have learned that he is a regular fellow. Many of the officers stand in line with the boys at chow and await their turn. All militarism has been dropped, and things really are humming here. It's so much better for morale to be actually doing a job—a sensible job that the fellows realize the need for—instead of answering musters, sitting watches, saluting, drilling, etc. This experience makes you realize that there are a lot of damn good Americans who will do a hell of a lot of work if only given the opportunity. And if a fight comes along, these fellows can be depended on to the last man of us. We have a swell battalion, both officers and men.

"It's terribly damp here. It rains—rather it pours—two or three times every day, and it never misses a night. Our clothes, even though in our trunks, are mildewing and shoes are molding. The stamps that I have are mostly stuck fast to other papers, and the airmail envelopes are glued tightly together, so that I have to put them into hot water to get them open. And you should smell my moldy mattress! But we like it and get along swell, even though it does rain. Let it rain—who cares? Tojo can't aim very well in a rainstorm.

"Luckily, this is one of the few islands not infested with mosquitoes. But ants, lizards, snakes, bugs and flies are troublesome—in that order. I've noticed a lot of great large white parrots with topknots. I'd like to catch one, a baby one, and bring it home. They are the prettiest things, flying around wild. They say the natives know how to catch them, so perhaps I can get them to bring me one for a few bars of candy or a pack of cigarettes. I'm not sure I would be allowed to bring it home, but it won't hurt to try!"

Frederick LaTour, Photographer's Mate second, Pasadena, Cal., of the Fourth Detachment, Second Battalion, was in the first detachment to land at Funafuti in the Ellice Islands. He reported: "We charged ashore, covered by B-17's, but the Japs had gone. We were given thirty-two hours to unload our gear and supplies, then the ship dashed off during an alert and carried most of our food. We lived on Vienna sausage and hardtack for five weeks.

"The island of Funafuti is seven miles long and 500 feet wide on the average. It is a coral island with no elevations more than a few feet above sea level. There is no fresh water and scant vegetation. The natives are handsome and show a Caucasian strain, having intermarried with the O'Brien family. They have a high sense of morality. The Seabees brought the first wheels ever to touch the island. Civilization is just beginning to spoil the natives. Before we came there was no money; and the natives used bright cloth and woven mats as currency."

LaTour described one of the many types of diving done by the Seabees in the South Pacific.

"At Funafuti," he said, "we had a lot of underwater work to do in connection with building the seaplane base. I helped with the diving when I wasn't busy on progress photographs. We used the shallow-diving mask for all work no deeper than thirty feet. Our first job was to clean the 'niggerheads' out of the entire operations area in the bay. These 'niggerheads' are mushroom-like coral deposits on the ocean floor, and they have to be blown out, so they won't obstruct planes. They are anywhere from ten to twenty feet tall, so we'd go down and place four or five cases of dynamite, and the blasts would crush the 'niggerheads' so that they'd settle.

"All we had to worry about was sharks. One day I was down placing dynamite; I was naked except for my shallow-diving mask and a thin Manila line around my waist. Sometimes I would stay down an hour and place twenty-five or thirty cases. Suddenly, the boys in the whaleboat gave two yanks on my line—the signal to come up. Ordinarily, I would take four or five minutes to come up, but something told me to go fast this time. I jerked off my helmet and the water smacked hell out of my eardrums, but I went shooting up to the surface.

"Right behind me were two sharks, one about eighteen and the other about twelve feet long. The fellows pulled me in the boat just a split second before the sharks could grab me. The sharks had been attracted by my bubbles—the bubbles fascinate them—and had I come up with my helmet on, they would have got me sure. None of our boys got hurt by the sharks, but many of the natives have hands and legs off as the result of shark battles."

It was to Funafuti that Captain Rickenbacker was brought after being picked up by a Navy patrol plane.

Dee Harden, of Arlington, Va., Chief Carpenter's Mate with the Bobcat Detachment at Bora Bora, wrote letters to his wife each week. Here are some excerpts over an eighteen-month period.

JULY 26, 1942

"JUST FINISHED MY LAUNDRY. CAN YOU IMAGINE USING LUX SOAP FOR DUNGAREES? I WAS LUCKY ENOUGH TO HAVE THREE BARS, BUT IT WAS SOME JOB TRYING TO WASH MUD AND GREASE OUT OF DUNGAREES WITH A BEAUTY SOAP. HOWEVER, WHEN THAT IS ALL YOU HAVE YOU JUST MAKE THE MOST OF IT AND GRIPE. I WISH THOSE DIETITIANS HAD TO EAT THAT CANNED STUFF THEY GIVE US.

PERHAPS THEY WOULDN'T THINK IT WAS SO GOOD. A SHIP PUT IN HERE RECENTLY AND WE HAD SOME REAL EGGS, NOT POWDERED. ALSO, WE HAD OUR FIRST FRESH MEAT—ROAST BEEF, FRESH POTATOES AND APPLES. OF COURSE, WE ONLY HAD ONE MEAL, BUT WE WERE DAMN GLAD TO GET THAT MUCH. WE KNOW THAT WE ARE HARD UP FOR SHIPS, AND AS LONG AS WE GET SOMETHING, WE ARE LUCKY AND THANKFUL."

AUGUST 2, 1942

"EVERYONE FEELS IN HIGH SPIRITS TONIGHT. WE JUST HAD WORD WE WERE GOING HOME FOR A REST VERY SOON. IT SEEMS TOO GOOD TO BE TRUE."

NOVEMBER 30, 1942

"THIS IS A GOOD DAY TO WRITE. IT'S SUNDAY AND RAINING CATS AND DOGS. I WENT TO CHURCH AT SEVEN, THEN ATE BREAKFAST AND DID SOME WASHING. WE REALLY HAVEN'T TOO MUCH TO COMPLAIN ABOUT EXCEPT THE COMPLETE LACK OF LIBERTY. WE HAVEN'T HAD A CHANCE TO GET AWAY FROM ANY OF THIS SINCE WE LANDED TEN MONTHS AGO.

I GUESS WE AREN'T SO BAD OFF, IF ONLY THOSE DAMN RUMORS ABOUT GOING HOME DIDN'T GET STARTED. AGAIN, WE HAVE

*BEEN PROMISED THAT WE WILL BE SENT HOME, AND WE ARE
AGAIN BUILDING UP HIGH HOPES. IT WAS A LONELY
THANKSGIVING, BUT THE MEAL WAS GOOD. TURKEY, SMOKED
HAM, SWEET POTATOES, COLESLAW, PICKLES, DRESSING, HOT
ROLLS, PUDDING AND ICE CREAM. EACH ONE OF US RECEIVED
CANDY AND CIGARETTES FROM SOME CARPENTERS' LOCAL IN
BALTIMORE. I HAVE A NECKLACE FOR YOU BUT WILL KEEP IT
AND HOPE I CAN DELIVER IT IN PERSON SOON."*

DECEMBER 15, 1942

*"HAVE BEEN READING SOME OF THAT PUBLICITY STUFF ABOUT
THE SEABEES BEING THE GLAMOUR BOYS OF THE NAVY. WE
SURE RIDICULE SUCH NONSENSE DOWN HERE. PERHAPS THAT
GAG STUFF IS EXPECTED, BUT IT MAKES US SIT BACK AND
WONDER IF THE PEOPLE BACK HOME KNOW WHAT IT IS ALL
ABOUT. IT'S TOO BAD A BOMB CAN'T BE DROPPED IN THE FRONT
YARD OF ALL THOSE FLAG WAVERS WHO JUST SIT PRETTY AND
LOOK CUTE. MAKE NO MISTAKE ABOUT IT, THERE IS NO
ROMANCE, GLAMOUR OR GLORY TO ANY OF THIS ROTTEN MESS.
WE ARE FACING NAKED FACTS, AND THE WONDER OF IT ALL IS
HOW WE MANAGED TO SURVIVE THE FIRST TWO MONTHS OF
THIS HELL, MUCH LESS A YEAR OF IT. WE DO, HOWEVER, HAVE
THE PERSONAL SATISFACTION OF KNOWING THAT WE ARE DOING
A MIGHTY BIG JOB DOWN HERE AND MAKING IT A DAMN GOOD
ONE. BUT I DO GET BURNED UP AT WHAT I HEAR OVER THE
RADIO AND READ IN THE NEWSPAPERS."*

DECEMBER 25, 1942

*"WELL, IT'S XMAS DAY AND NOTHING TO DO. AM WRITING IN
THE VICTORY HUT. THERE WAS SO MUCH RACKET IN OUR OWN
HUT THAT I COULDN'T THINK, SO I CAME DOWN HERE TO WRITE
YOU. IT'S RAINING AGAIN. I GOT OUT AT SIX AND WENT TO
CHURCH AT SEVEN, THEN JUST KILLED TIME UNTIL TWELVE.
HAD OUR CHOW AND IT WAS ABOUT THE SAME AS
THANKSGIVING. I WOULD HAVE PREFERRED TO WORK TODAY
BECAUSE THE TIME PASSES SO MUCH QUICKER, AND THIS XMAS
WOULD HAVE BEEN OVER BEFORE I HAD TIME TO THINK TOO
MUCH ABOUT IT. THERE WAS QUITE A CELEBRATION AT THE
MOVIE HUT LAST NIGHT. WE DIDN'T HAVE TAPS UNTIL TWELVE.
I WOULD CELEBRATE, TOO, IF I HAD ANYTHING TO CELEBRATE,
BUT I DON'T LIKE THESE HANGOVERS DOWN HERE. BESIDES,
IT'S TOO MUCH TROUBLE TO GET ANYTHING TO DRINK. IF A*

PERSON CAN ONLY KEEP GOING AND KEEP HIS MIND OCCUPIED,
HE CAN GET BY ALL RIGHT."

JANUARY 1, 1943

"IT'S NEW YEAR'S, AND I DIDN'T THINK ABOUT IT UNTIL WE HAD
CHICKEN FOR CHOW. WE ARE GETTING MORE FRESH
VEGETABLES AND FRESH MEAT LATELY. WE DID HAVE SUCH
TERRIBLE FOOD FOR SUCH A LONG TIME, AND SO MANY TIMES
WE HAD TO WORK AWFULLY HARD ON EMPTY STOMACHS
BECAUSE WE COULDN'T EAT THE FOOD. I DON'T THINK I'LL
EVER BE ABLE TO LOOK SPAM OR VIENNA SAUSAGE IN THE
FACE AGAIN, BUT THANK GOD, MOST OF THAT'S OVER NOW."

MARCH 9, 1943

"WE HAVE A LOT OF CHRONIC BRONCHITIS DOWN HERE, DUE TO
BEING SO CLOSE TO SEA LEVEL. THE GROUND OUTSIDE OUR
HUT IS ABOUT EIGHT FEET ABOVE SEA LEVEL, SO IT'S A GOOD
THING IT IS ALWAYS CALM. LAST WEEK WE BOARDED UP THE
ENDS OF THE HUTS AND NAILED EVERYTHING DOWN EXPECTING
A HURRICANE, BUT WE ONLY GOT THE TAIL END OF IT.

"WE SURE WERE LUCKY BECAUSE I WOULD HATE TO SEE ALL
THIS WORK RUINED NOW. HAVE SOME BEAUTIFUL SHELLS FOR
YOU. WE GATHER THE SHELLS AND BURY THEM UNDER THE HUT
AND LET THE ANTS EAT THE INSIDES OUT, AND THEN WE WASH
THEM OUT. THE NATIVES TAKE THESE SMALL SHELLS AND USE
THEM FOR BUTTONS. WHEN THEY ARE MATCHED THEY MAKE
VERY UNIQUE BUTTONS. PERHAPS I CAN DO SOMETHING WITH
THE ONES I HAVE FOR YOU."

APRIL 15, 1943

"AM NOW IN THE CAMOUFLAGE DIVISION AND LIKE IT VERY
MUCH. IT'S SURPRISING HOW EASILY THE SHRUBS AND VINES
GROW. WE JUST HACK THEM OFF AND STICK THE BRANCHES IN
THE GROUND AND THEY KEEP ON GROWING. THIS CERTAINLY IS
A BEAUTIFUL PLACE.

"THE COMBINATION OF COLORED FLYING FISH, CORAL, CLOUDS,
THE SEA, AND THE SUN SHINING DOWN IN A RAINBOW OF

COLORS MAKES THE PICTURES YOU SEE IN THE MOVIES LOOK
DULL. IT'S TOO BAD WE MUST BE HERE IN WARTIME AND SPOIL
SO MUCH OF THE NATURAL BEAUTY."

MAY 12, 1943

"HERE IS ANOTHER PAGE FOR OUR MEMORY BOOK. SOME OF
US WENT TO A NEARBY ISLAND TO WATCH THE FIRE DANCE.
THE NATIVES HAD A LARGE PIT ABOUT FOUR FEET DEEP FILLED
WITH BURNING LOGS AND COVERED WITH ROCKS. ABOUT EIGHT
O'CLOCK THE SO-CALLED DANCE STARTED. ABOUT TEN
COUPLES TOOK PART IN IT WITH A LEADER. EACH PERSON HELD
A TORCH. THE LEADER TOOK A LARGE BUNCH OF PALM LEAVES,
AND AFTER A LOT OF GIBBERISH WHICH THEY CALL TALKING
WITH THEIR GODS, HE BEGAN MAKING MOTIONS LIKE A PERSON
DODGING TRAFFIC. THEN HE BEAT THE STONES WITH THE PALM
LEAVES AND WALKED ACROSS THE HOT STONES. ALL THE
NATIVES WENT INTO A CHANT, AND ONE OF THE GIRLS
PERFORMED SOME SORT OF HULA DANCE, AND THE TEN
COUPLES WALKED BACK AND FORTH ACROSS THE HOT STONES.
ALL THE NATIVES JUMPED UP AND STARTED DANCING ACROSS
THE HOT STONES. THE NEXT THING WE KNEW A LOT OF
SOLDIERS AND SAILORS WERE IN THE CIRCLE JUST YELLING LIKE
COMANCHES AND DANCING TO BEAT HELL. WE GOT THE HELL
OUT OF THERE."

MAY 30, 1943

"AM STILL SHARK FISHING FOR RECREATION. WE HAVE HAD
CONSIDERABLE LUCK. THE DAMN SHARKS BENT ALL MY HOOKS,
BUT I FINALLY MADE ONE THAT COULD BE USED FOR AN
ANCHOR IN THE POTOMAC. LAST SUNDAY WE CAUGHT FOUR BIG
SHARKS. THREE OF US WENT OUT AFTER CHOW LAST NIGHT
AND CAUGHT FOURTEEN FISH ABOUT TEN INCHES LONG, AND
THEN WE HAD A FISH FRY. IT SURE TASTED GOOD."

JUNE 12, 1943

"YOU ASKED ABOUT THE NATIVES AND ALL THE MONEY THEY
TAKE IN. THERE ARE TWO OR THREE CHINESE STORES, AND
THEY CARRY A SMALL LINE OF CANNED GOODS, STRAW HATS,

BELTS, KEROSENE LAMPS AND LANTERNS. I SAW SOME SMALL CANS OF PAINT WITH A LABEL MARKED 'GLIDDEN COMPANY, CLEVELAND.' ONE CHINK HAS STARTED A BAKERY AND MAKES GOOD BREAD BUT NOT ENOUGH OF IT. ANOTHER CHINK HAS A MODEL A FORD AND TAKES THE NATIVES FOR A RIDE FOR FIFTY CENTS PER PERSON. I HAVE SEEN SOME OF THESE NATIVES WITH FIVE-GALLON CANS STUFFED FULL OF FOLDING MONEY, AND THEY DON'T KNOW WHAT TO DO WITH IT. THEY WILL GIVE $300 FOR A WRISTWATCH.

WE ARE GROWING A GARDEN IN A SMALL WAY, BUT IT MUST BE BOARDED UP OR THE CRABS WOULD EAT IT RIGHT DOWN TO THE GROUND. THESE DAMN CRABS CRAWL SIDEWAYS AND GO LIKE A BAT OUT OF HELL. THEY EVEN CLIMB THE COCONUT TREES."

JUNE 25, 1943

"THREE OF US HAVE SPENT OUR SUNDAYS PAINTING THE CHAPEL. IT BELONGS TO THE NATIVES, AND THE LOCAL MISSIONARY PRIEST, FATHER VENANCE, WAS SO PLEASED ABOUT IT THAT HE INSISTED ON GIVING US SOME BEADS AND TRINKETS. THIS MISSIONARY HAS SO LITTLE TO WORK ON AND LIVES SO POORLY THAT WE DIDN'T WANT TO TAKE ANYTHING FROM HIM, BUT HE WAS SO INSISTENT THAT WE TOOK THE TRINKETS AS A REMEMBRANCE, "I'M SAVING THEM FOR YOU."

JULY 15, 1943

"FINALLY GOT MY CHIEF'S RATING, SO NOW I DON'T HAVE TO BUCK THE CHOW LINE ANYMORE. I HAVE ONLY A MAKESHIFT UNIFORM. THE CAP I WEAR HAS QUITE A HISTORY. I TRADED EIGHT CANS OF BEER FOR IT, SINCE BEER WILL BUY THINGS THAT MONEY WON'T DOWN HERE. WENT TO CHURCH SERVICES IN A LAUNCH LAST SUNDAY. FATHER VENANCE IS THE ONLY CHAPLAIN ON THE ISLAND NOW. HE HAS BEEN STUDYING HIS ENGLISH SINCE WE HAVE BEEN ON THE ISLAND. THERE WAS A TIME WHEN WE COULDN'T UNDERSTAND HIM, BUT NOW HE CAN BAWL HELL OUT OF US AND MAKE US UNDERSTAND."

AUGUST 12, 1943

"IF YOU WERE DISAPPOINTED BECAUSE WE DIDN'T GET BACK, JUST THINK HOW IT WAS ON US TO HAVE TO WATCH THAT BOAT COME IN AND THEN SHOVE OFF WITHOUT US. IT JUST ABOUT TORE THE HEARTS OUT OF EVERY ONE OF US DOWN HERE. JUST THINK, A YEAR AGO WE THOUGHT WE'D BE GOING HOME WITHIN A FEW DAYS! I AM ENCLOSING $200 IN BETS MADE BY SCATES, BAYNE AND WALSH. [KENNETH SCATES, PAINTER FIRST; ROBERT BAYNE, MACHINIST'S MATE FIRST; AND BERNARD WALSH, GUNNER'S MATE SECOND, ALL OF WASHINGTON, D.C.] IF GERMANY IS STILL IN THE WAR BY THE END OF THE YEAR, SEND THE MONEY TO SCATES'S MOTHER; BUT IF NOT, SPLIT IT BETWEEN BAYNE AND WALSH."

OCTOBER 1, 1943

"WELL, WE ARE ON THE MOVE AGAIN, BUT IN THE WRONG DIRECTION! WE MUST BE DAMNED IMPORTANT PEOPLE, OR PERHAPS IT'S THE OTHER WAY AROUND. WE SURE GET PUSHED AROUND. AFTER BEING WITH THE ARMY ALL THOSE MONTHS, WE ARE NOW WITH THE MARINES. THE NATIVES WEAR SKIRTS HERE. THE BIRDS START SINGING ABOUT 4:30 IN THE MORNING AND YOU SHOULD HEAR THE RACKET

MUCH RAIN HAS FALLEN LATELY, AND WE HAVE A TOUGH TIME TRYING TO KEEP OUR CLOTHES DRY. ANYTHING WITH LEATHER ON IT MOLDS OVERNIGHT, THEN ROTS IMMEDIATELY. WE MUST CLEAN OUR RIFLES AT LEAST EVERY OTHER DAY."

DECEMBER 25, 1943

"WELL, HERE IS ANOTHER CHRISTMAS. IT'S MY THIRD CHRISTMAS AWAY FROM HOME AND YOU. REMEMBER HOW I ENLISTED SO QUICKLY AFTER PEARL HARBOR? AND THEN I DIDN'T GET TO COME HOME BEFORE WE SHOVED OFF. I GOT THE PIPE YOU SENT ME. THIS MORNING I GOT UP EARLY, PUT ON MY CLEAN SUIT AND WENT TO CHURCH. NOW I AM SMOKING MY NEW PIPE AND TRYING NOT TO THINK TOO MUCH. YOU JUST CAN'T THINK ABOUT THE NICE THINGS AT HOME AND THE THINGS YOU ARE MISSING AND STILL BE IN THE RIGHT FRAME OF MIND TO FIGHT THE JAPS. I JUST PUT ALL THOSE THOUGHTS IN

THE CORNER OF MY MIND AND CLOSE THE DOOR ON IT. IF I'M LUCKY AND COME OUT OF THIS ALIVE, THEN WHEN IT'S ALL OVER I'LL JUST OPEN THE DOOR ON MY THOUGHTS—BUT NOT BEFORE. SOUNDS SIMPLE, DOESN'T IT, BUT IT'S A LOT HARDER TO PUT INTO PRACTICE.

THERE ARE PLENTY OF THINGS THAT I NEVER MENTION THAT ARE ENOUGH TO DRIVE ANYONE CRAZY IF HE DOESN'T MANAGE TO LOOK AT IT RIGHT. BELIEVE ME, WE BOBCATS ARE THE GREATEST MORALE BUSTERS IN THE ENTIRE PACIFIC. EVERY PLACE WE GO WE RUN UP AGAINST SEABEES AND OTHERS WHO HAVE BEEN OUT HERE ANYWHERE FROM SIX MONTHS TO A YEAR, AND THEY ALL HAVE BRIGHT VISIONS OF GOING HOME 'BY CHRISTMAS' OR AT LEAST IN THE NEXT SIXTY OR NINETY DAYS. AND THEN WE COME ALONG AND TELL THEM WE'VE BEEN HERE TWO YEARS WITH STILL NO RELIEF IN SIGHT.

"WHEN WE COME AROUND THEY ALL SHUT UP LIKE CLAMS NOW. ONE OF THE CHIEFS WAS TELLING ME THAT HIS GANG WAS ALWAYS RAISING HELL AND TALKING OF ALL THE CELEBRATING THEY WOULD BE DOING BACK IN THE STATES IN A FEW SHORT WEEKS. BUT NOW THAT THEY HAVE SEEN US THEY ARE AS MEEK AS LAMBS AND READY TO BREAK DOWN AND CRY. WELL, I GUESS IF OUR GANG CAN'T TAKE IT, NO ONE CAN. I'VE ALWAYS HAD A HIGH REGARD FOR THE MARINES, BUT OUR BOYS WILL MATCH THEM MAN FOR MAN.

"PERHAPS IT'S OUR ABILITY TO GET THINGS DONE WHEN THE CHIPS ARE DOWN THAT HAS GOT US WHERE WE ARE NOW. I DON'T KNOW IF YOU'D CONSIDER THAT GOOD OR BAD. WE HAVE OUR OWN OPINION. I THOUGHT I'D BE ABLE TO SEND YOU A SURPRISE WIRE FOR CHRISTMAS, BUT THEY WOULDN'T LET ME DO IT. WELL, I'LL HAVE TO BE GETTING ON WITH THE WAR. THIS CAN'T LAST FOREVER—OR CAN IT?"

7: The Magic Box of the Seabees

WHEN MILITARY HISTORIANS ANALYZE ALL THE complex machinery with which this war was won, they may decide that a simple steel box contributed as much to the victory as either radar or the Sperry bombsight. This box is the Navy pontoon, a five-by-seven-by-five-foot cube of sheet steel which, multiplied and handled like toy building blocks, can become a landing barge, a pier, a causeway or a floating drydock right under the enemy's startled eyes. How it was developed by the Civil Engineer Corps and how the Seabees used it to make possible our victories in the Mediterranean is another thrilling story of American ingenuity.

This magic box was the horseshoe nail which made possible our landings in Sicily and at Salerno and Anzio. The Germans never expected us to land where and when we did in southern Sicily. They figured one physical factor would stop us: shallow water off the beaches. Where water deepens at a normal rate, our LST's can drive their ramps clear to the beach, and our machines can rumble ashore with no loss of time. But the beach situation along much of southern Sicily is abnormal. Five hundred feet from the shore around Licata, Sicily, the LST's would ground on the gently sloping bottom, yet the water would still be six feet deep at their ramps. We'd have a perilous ship-to-shore problem; so, assuming that we'd never risk such a situation under their bombs, the Germans prepared to meet our attack farther north.

Shortly after our landing in North Africa, Allied experts began wrestling with the problem. How could we get tanks, bulldozers and trucks within "wading distance" of that beach? Two hundred feet from the shore the water became shallow enough for the vehicles to "wade" on matting. But that still left 300 feet of too deep water in front of our ramps, a distance that would have to be bridged with not more than a thirty-minute delay. How could this be done?

The Army Engineers began experimenting with their famous steel treadways, laid across rubber doughnuts. In the Navy the problem was referred to Captain John N. Laycock, a soft-voiced, circumspect Yankee from Massachusetts who smokes ten-cent corncob pipes and makes war plans for the CEC. Designer of the Navy pontoon and all its tricky gear, Captain Laycock had already performed feats of pontoon magic. He had discovered ways to fasten the steel boxes together in several useful combinations; and he knew how to keep these pontoon assemblies rigid and capable of sustaining great weight in a heavy sea. But there were limits to the length and size of these pontoon assemblies.

"To make a steel causeway wide enough for tanks and trucks," Captain Laycock explained, "we would have to fasten two pontoons together to get a width of a little more than 14 feet. (Remember each pontoon is cube five feet by seven feet by five feet deep.) Then we could extend the length of the causeway by adding two-pontoon sections until we reached the maximum safe length. Of course, the longer the structure became the more flexible it became, and the more likely to break up under stress. We believed that about 105 feet was about our maximum length for a two pontoon-wide causeway. To make the causeways longer would mean going into our factor of safety. A 300-foot causeway seemed out of the question. However, we began experimenting with longer causeways; and we found that 175-foot structures were flexible, but they could withstand considerable stress.

"Then we hit upon the slide-rule idea. If a 300-foot structure was too long and too flexible to withstand surf action, why not use two 175-foot assemblies, overlap them and make their combined length adjustable? We set the Seabees to practicing with such an arrangement, and then we arranged a dual demonstration."

That demonstration determined our tactics in Sicily. Indeed, it determined our LST landing tactics for this war. Somewhere along Narragansett Bay two LST's, carrying distinguished British and American observers, approached a beach at full speed. Aboard one of the LST's were the Army Engineers, ready to go into action with their treadways and rubber doughnuts. Aboard the other LST were the Seabees, and they were towing their two 175-foot pontoon assemblies with men riding the pontoons. The two 175-foot sections were being towed alongside the LST, and the sections were in the slide-rule position: they rode side by side, fastened together, with one section slightly in advance of the other.

Suddenly, 500 feet from the shore, both ships grounded, and action flared. The Engineers dropped their front ramp, began throwing their doughnuts over the side and pushing their treadways out of the open bow—just as the Engineers cross a freshwater stream. But the Seabees were doing tricks. As the Seabee LST began to ground, the men on the pontoon causeways had cut them loose and allowed them to drive on toward the beach without losing momentum. The forward end of the leading causeway section was run into two-foot water and grounded; then the Seabees pulled a second trick. The stern end of the trailing pontoon section had a line on it from the LST, and by quickly unlocking the two pontoon sections and hauling this line, the Seabees lengthened their pontoon "slide rule" until the second string was pulled back to the LST ramp and made fast. Where the two 175-foot sections overlapped, they were quickly clamped together again.

In just seven minutes after the Seabee LST had grounded, a huge anti-tank gun charged out of the bow doors, crossed the fourteen-foot-wide steel causeway, "waded" the shallow water and reached the beach!

"Army and Navy officers seldom gasp," said Captain Laycock, "but we all gasped at that demonstration. We knew that we had a surprise for the Germans."

That was March 18, 1943. Within twenty-four hours a trainload of pontoons pulled out of Davisville, R.I. Great piles of these gray steel boxes accumulated along the North African Coast. The Seabees had another hurry-up job on their hands— the job of guaranteeing that wherever our LST's ground, our men, tanks and trucks can reach shore quickly. The Pontoon Detachments, made up of picked officers and men, were created and trained. In North Africa, as well as along our own Eastern seaboard, these detachments practiced day and night. Endlessly, they rehearsed the trick of driving the heavy pontoon assemblies ashore—a locomotive shunting cars into a siding.

Ninety-six 175-foot pontoon causeways were assembled in North Africa—a total of 5,760 pontoons. For transportation to the landing scene, Rear Admiral Richard L. Conolly, commanding American landing craft in Africa, thought that the pontoon causeway should be slung on the sides of the LST's rather than towed, and this method was tried. It enabled the convoy to move faster. Then, on the July night when the great armada set sail for Sicily, the pontoon causeways went first. Some of them were being towed by tugs; others were carried by the LST's in the new side-carry manner.

Next morning, German pilots looked down on the southern beaches and rubbed their eyes. What couldn't happen was happening. Standing 500 feet out in the water, the fat American craft were disgorging vehicles by the hundreds! As fast as one LST was unloaded, the Seabees would unfasten the causeway and swing it around to a waiting ship. Over these smooth steel causeways, the Pontoon Detachment unloaded a total of 11,500 vehicles.

When General Sir Bernard Law Montgomery stepped from his landing boat, a photographer grabbed the picture. "A picture for history the photographer said, "General Montgomery setting foot on Sicily." But Admiral Lord Louis Mountbatten corrected him. "The general is not setting foot on Sicily at the moment." Mountbatten pointed out. "He is setting foot on one of these miraculous American pontoons."

After the Sicilian invasion the Seabees labored to improve their causeway technique. The towing method was discarded for the side-carry method. This side-carry is accomplished by welding interlocking brackets on the ship and along one edge of the causeway. Then the ship is made to list sharply toward the causeway by flooding the ship's tanks on that side; the brackets are interlocked; the causeway is leaned on its edge against the LST and secured; then the water is expelled from the tanks, and the ship rights herself, lifting the causeway clear. The same process is repeated on the other side of the ship, and she has picked up her two causeway sections and is ready to disgorge her cargo on even the flattest of beaches.

Besides allowing the convoy to move faster, the side-carry technique exposes a smaller area of causeway to enemy bombs. When being towed the causeway, sections offer a twenty-nine-foot-wide target flat in the water, but when being carried on edge they offer only five-foot dimensions of the two sections.

Each LST carrying causeways has a Seabee pontoon platoon of two officers and thirty-four men. When the LST arrives three or four miles off the invasion beach, Seabees with axes stand along the decks and, at a signal, they cut the cables holding the causeway sections, and the causeways hit the water with a great splash. The Seabees then open the bow doors, lower the ramp, and "let the duck out." An amphibious tractor drives out into the water. Using the "duck" for towing purposes, the Seabees then maneuver the two sections into the slide-rule position along one side of the LST, and the ship starts its run toward the beach. One officer and twenty-four Seabees are lying belly-down on the causeways as the LST makes its run. The LST grounds at full speed, and the causeways, with a terrific way on, cut loose at exactly the proper second, stream onto the beach to be rigged with almost no loss of time. It's the slickest trick of the war.

The men who ride these plunging causeways through a heavy surf, with bombs, shells and mines exploding around them, claim that they are the toughest of all the Seabees. Unarmed and with no cover, they are as exposed as frogs on a flat rock. At Salerno and Anzio, the Germans were expecting the causeways, so we suffered casualties from countermeasures. By concentrating on the causeways, German bombardiers were able to break some of them. But despite heavy casualties, the Seabees unloaded over 150 LST's at Salerno and did even better at Anzio—as will be detailed in the following chapter.

The causeway has vastly complicated the German defense problem. Before we developed it, there were long reaches off at coastline which the Germans could leave unprotected. Nature alone would keep away anything stronger than patrols, and the Germans could concentrate at the favorable beaches. But with the causeway we can land and supply whole armies over the flattest of beaches.

Yet the causeway is the magic pontoon in only one of its resultant forms. Assemble the pontoons in a second combination, add an outboard propulsion unit, and you get a self-propelled barge. Use a third pattern and you get a floating drydock. A fourth pattern gives you a seaplane ramp; a fifth, a pier; a sixth, a buoy. New useful combinations are still being discovered, and each combination is contributing to victory as I shall explain subsequently.

In their first Pacific role, the pontoon causeways played a brave part in the victory at Kwajalein in the Marshalls. There, as at most atolls, the landing problem was the coral shelf which surrounds the islets. Water depth on these shelves varies with the tides, and uncharted coral "heads" along the shelves are a further hazard for the charging LST's. No one can be certain just where the big landing craft will grind to a halt, but the adjustable causeways insure us against delay, whatever happens.

A flanking maneuver at Kwajalein islet saved the life of many an Attu veteran of the Army's Seventh Division. Before the Seventh assaulted Kwajalein itself, heavy howitzers were landed first on Carlson islet, which lies two miles off the northwest end of Kwajalein. This landing was accomplished early on D-Day when Lieutenant Commander Jack McGaraghan (CEC, USNR, Eureka, Cal.) and his Seabee detachment laid a causeway against Carlson. With the causeway and amphibious tractors to supply the guns, artillerymen began blasting the Jap positions on Kwajalein and were able to provide close cover for the assault troops.

After positions had been secured on Kwajalein, the Seabees went into the lagoon, laid four causeways against the islet, and unloaded the heavy equipment for repairing the airstrip. One of the LST's hung on a coral head so far out in the lagoon that it could be unloaded only by a ferry technique. Using a 175-foot string as the ferry over 500 feet of water, the Seabees would haul the string back to the LST ramp with a winch, load it with vehicles, then haul the string clear on the beach with a bulldozer. This method, as old as the backcountry river ferry, was still good enough to unload the LST in two hours.

As early as 1936, the Civil Engineer Corps had foreseen that a Pacific conflict would demand great quantities of new devices for beach operations. Land bases would be the decisive element. This meant the handling of unprecedented amounts of supplies over all sorts of beaches. It meant myriads of small, specialized craft; floating piers; self-propelled barges; floating bases for cranes; and portable, floating dry docks to service all these light craft. It meant the development of a whole new science of beach operations.

It was not until 1940, however, that Captain Laycock injected the revolutionary note into this beach thinking. Since floating piers, drydocks, causeways and barges would be needed in such numbers, why not devise one section which could be prefabricated and made the basic part of all this beach equipment?

The inevitable reaction was that it couldn't be done. To be strong, rigid and capable of sustaining great weight, a barge had to be a unit—a welded, riveted unit. How could a sectional barge be made rigid? True, the Germans had built small sectional barges, but the sections, called catamarans, were ponderous affairs with many objectionable features. The catamaran was not for us.

But suppose this single unit—this magic box—could be devised? And, more important, suppose a way could be discovered by which the rigidity of one box could be imparted to a combination of boxes? It was a problem to challenge the most agile engineering brains in the country. If such a box could be designed, then America's problem of making war at great distance would be simplified. No longer would we have to build barges and drydocks at home and then tow them across oceans. Instead, we could ship the components of the magic box to our advance bases; assemble the boxes; then barges, piers, drydocks and causeways could spring full-blown almost within rifle shot of the enemy.

For months during 1940, the CEC sought to interest private manufacturers in the idea. In December 1940, Captain Laycock devoted part of his leave to a trip to Pittsburgh to implore a barge manufacturer to begin experiment. But the country was not at war; we were still fighting imaginary battles; so, negotiations moved slowly.

Captain Laycock's answer was to come back to Washington and begin collecting cigar boxes. For weeks he had every concessionaire in the Navy Building saving empty cigar boxes for him. He arranged these boxes in many combinations, and with them he worked out his method by which many boxes can be bolted together, and the resulting structure can be almost as strong as if it were one piece.

By February 1941, Captain Laycock had put his basic unit—the pontoon—on paper. Its top dimensions were five feet by seven feet, and it was five feet deep. Built of sheet steel, it weighed approximately 2,600 pounds. The magic "jewelry"—the self-tightening, interlocking bolts and straps which connected the boxes—weighed another 100 pounds per pontoon. Three structures to be built from the boxes were designed: a 50-ton barge, a 100-ton dry dock, and a seaplane ramp. A contract for these experimental structures was signed with the Pittsburgh-Des Moines Steel Company on February 18, 1941.

Simultaneously, Murray & Tregurtha, boatbuilders, of North Quincy, Mass., began building an outboard propulsion unit; and the first of these units was ready to be tested, along with the other structures, late in the spring of 1941. The tests, held on the Ohio River at Pittsburgh, were completely successful. The British were so delighted that they placed an immediate order for 3,000 pontoons at $700 each.

Since then the manufacture of the pontoon and its jewelry has become a major industry. Seventy-five firms are now building many thousands of pontoons a month. During 1944 about 240,000 tons of high-priority sheet steel will go into pontoons; and despite steady reductions in unit cost, the Navy will pay $100,000,000 for pontoon gear. The jewelry, which at first had to be machined, is now stamped out in mass production. Assembly of the pontoons and the pontoon structures is a huge military enterprise conducted by the Seabees across the seas.

The first dramatic test for the pontoons was at Ascension Island. This little dot in the South Atlantic, situated halfway between the Brazilian and African humps, has been one of the world's most valuable pieces of real estate to the American war effort. For three years it was hidden behind a thick screen of censorship, but the censors have now admitted the revelation that an airstrip on Ascension made possible outflow of air commerce to Africa, the Middle East and India. What is revealed here is that it was the pontoon which made possible the "conquest" of Ascension.

Ascension was defended by neither Germans nor Japs, but by Nature rampant. In a forbidding atmosphere of strong trade winds, the South Atlantic meets the North Atlantic at Ascension; and, even in normal weather, waves beat eleven feet high against its rocky beach. To land heavy equipment on Ascension would take the best of American seamanship.

Since it was to be an Army project, a sturdy detachment of Engineers practiced with the Seabees and learned to handle pontoons. Then, on a wild March morning in 1942, the Engineers stormed Ascension. It was a rough show. They dropped a pontoon barge over a freighter's side, and the barge promptly tore a hole in the ship, so fierce was the wave action.

With superhuman effort, the Engineers finally lashed a bulldozer to the barge, then headed for the beach. It was the fifty-ton barge, which is three pontoons wide by seven longs. If those twenty-one pontoons could hold together at Ascension, they could hold together anywhere. After a terrific battering, the Engineers finally rammed the barge shard against the rocky reef that the bulldozer broke its lashings and was virtually catapulted onto the beach.

In the days that followed the Engineers fought the sea savagely. They rigged a small crane on a log pier, then struggled to bring the barges near enough the pier so that the equipment could be lifted to the beach. It was impossible to moor the barges alongside the pier. Every barge trip was a battle. The waves would hurl the barges against the ships, the pontoons would be crushed, but the sectional pattern kept the barges afloat. The barges enabled the Engineers to conquer Ascension; but, even now, with all our improvements there, landing supplies at Ascension is a tough job of seamanship.

The PT boats swelled the demand for pontoons. Like all these craft which operate near and off beaches, the PT's must be picked up often for repairs to their rudders and screws. With the Japs racing through the islands, some method for fast drydocking had to be evolved quickly. The pontoons provided a ready-made answer.

The pontoon box is fitted with pipes so that water can be let into the box, and later the water can be forced out with compressed air. To assemble the drydock the Seabees put forty-eight pontoons together in the barge pattern; then added upright pontoons to stabilize the barge while it was submerged. The PT boat approached the barge; water was let into the pontoons; the barge sank to the necessary depth, stabilized by the upright pontoons; the PT pulled in between the uprights; water was forced out of the pontoons with compressed air; and—*presto!*—the PT rose out of the water, sitting comfortably in its cradle, ready for repairs!

The trick is even more amazing than the causeways. Drydocking ships has always required skilled men and complex equipment. But, with the pontoons, the Navy now carries the drydocks along with it, and no particular skill is required. Our pontoon docks can repair any of our landing craft, up to and including the LST.

In still another form, the pontoons rescued the PT's during the terrible emergency in the South Pacific. With giant cranes the PT's were loaded on freighters in this country; but in the spring of

1942 there was not a crane at any of our bases in the South Pacific capable of lifting the PT's off the freighters.

It was one of those moments when one idea can turn the tide of battle. Working night and day, CEC officers designed a pontoon barge from which an enormous cantilever crane could operate. They loaded the pontoons and crane on a fast freighter at an Atlantic port and sent the freighter scurrying to the South Pacific. Then an awesome mistake was discovered. In rushing the blueprints for the crane, one young engineer had misread a dimension; and when the crane hoisted the PT, the hook would not be high enough to lift the boat clear.

Captain Laycock hastily explored the new problem. He examined the slings for lifting the boats and found that he could shorten them enough to compensate for the error, and the PT would clear the freighters rail. A night plane took off for Panama with blueprints for the new slings. Navy machine shops had the shorter slings ready to toss aboard the freighter when it eased into Gatun Locks. Movies, detailing how to assemble the barge and the crane, were flown to a Seabee battalion; and when the first PT's arrived off Noumea, New Caledonia, the high-hipped cantilever crane walked out to the freighter, reached up on her deck, hoisted the PT's, and deposited them safely in the water.

These were the PT's which helped win Guadalcanal.

In barge form, the pontoons are being used in vast numbers in the Pacific, as well as in the Mediterranean and around the British Isles. In the Pacific islands the war can almost be called a "barge war." The American public knows from our Pacific communiques that the Japs use hundreds of barges and that we have sunk hundreds of them. What is not so well known is that our forces, too, use hundreds of barges, and the pontoon gives us all the advantages in this type of competition.

We do not have to manufacture our barges at home and ship them overseas. We do not even have to complete the manufacture of the pontoons. We only have to stamp out the sheet steel sides of the pontoons at home; then we ship the knocked-down parts of the pontoons to advance bases where the Seabees complete the manufacture of the pontoons, then assemble the pontoons into barges. It's barges-while-you-wait at our advance bases in both the Pacific and the Atlantic.

We sink the Jap barges easily, yet we ourselves find it almost impossible to sink our pontoon barges with either bombs or gunfire. I have told how seven Seabees lost their lives when the Japs bombed a barge which was taking fuel from a destroyer at Guadalcanal. The incident occurred at night, and the flaming barge was aiding the Jap attack. The gas drums would shoot a hundred feet in the air, explode in a blaze of pyrotechnics, and light up the whole harbor. In an effort to put out the fire, Marine gunners began blasting at the barge with five-inch pieces. But it was no use. We couldn't sink our own barge. Next day, the Seabees simply patched a few pontoons, and the barge was good as new. It is still in use at Guadalcanal.

The Seabees who handle the pontoons are convinced that they can build anything with them. And after you visit Joe's Hamburger Stand in the South Pacific you are inclined to agree with them. Located just off an airstrip in the Russell Islands, Joe's serves up the most delicious hamburgers and hot cakes in that section of the world. And Joe's culinary secret is hidden in two pieces of improvised cooking equipment.

One is his bake oven—a battered pontoon with a door cut in its side, shelves installed and a gasoline burner under it. The other is his grill—a battered pontoon with a fire roaring inside it and hamburgers and hot cakes frying on its top surface.

121st NCB at Roi-Namur

(Feb 1, 1944)

8: Seabees at Salerno and in Sicily

THINK OF THE BEACH AROUND THE BAY AT Salerno as a twelve-mile arc. As you enter the bay, the town of Salerno is at the end of the arc on your left or north side. Moving your vision clockwise around the arc from Salerno, you see hills rolling back to become mountains; then on the southern half of the arc you see gently rolling, scrubby country, with an old stone tower breaking the landscape.

For purposes of the British-American landing at Salerno, the twelve-mile arc was divided into halves. The British were to land on North Beach; the Americans were to land on South Beach. North Beach was divided into two sections: Red and Green. It was known that the 16th Panzer Division was emplaced in the hills overlooking North Beach. It was thought that two Italian divisions were guarding South Beach; and since the Italians had surrendered, it was hoped that our operations on South Beach could move rapidly and that forces landed on South Beach could come very quickly to the assistance of our forces landing on North Beach.

Here was the landing plan: The vast invasion fleet, composed of everything from tiny LCVP's to heavy cruisers, would begin entering the bay shortly after midnight on September 9, 1943. At 0330 a detachment of Commandos and Raiders would begin landing in small craft on North Beach. Simultaneously, units of the 36th (Texas) Division would begin landing on South Beach. Minesweepers would be pushing behind the small landing craft so that the big LST's could come in and begin unloading as quickly thereafter as possible.

Among all our specialized landing craft, the LST is the ship that carries the punch. It's the big two-deck, 330-foot ship that disgorges heavy tanks, big guns and truck-and-trailer loads of ammunition and supplies. The small craft can put men ashore—men with grenades, flamethrowers and Bangalore torpedoes to knock out pillboxes and barbed wiremen to clear the mines and other obstructions on the beaches—but we can't really sock until the LST's can charge in, open their cavernous mouths and start vomiting the heavy stuff. Our troops on a beach can't advance very far against a prepared enemy until the LST's can land.

All of the LST's at Salerno were American and most were operated by the United States Navy. The British were landing the Eighth Army far to the south. But the LST's at Salerno which were to land at North Beach carried the 46th British Division, and those which were to land at South Beach carried the 36th American Division (formerly Texas National Guard).

The first six LST's which were to land at North Beach and the first four LST's which were to land at South Beach—these ten ships were carrying the pontoon causeways as the invasion fleet entered the bay. Aboard each of these ships was a platoon (two officers and thirty-four men) of Seabees to handle the causeways and rush the unloading. The causeway sections were the 175-foot sections described in the previous chapter. Each section weighed approximately ninety tons; and as each ship carried a causeway section slung on either side of it, this meant that each ship carried 160 tons of causeway. Also, as equipment for its Seabee platoon, each LST carried one "duck" and one bulldozer loaded on the forward end of its tank deck so that they could be first off the ship.

The first LST to go in to North Beach was Number 386, carrying Platoon 'C' of the 1006th C. B. Causeway Detachment led by Lieutenant Willis H. Mitchell (CEC, USNR, Long Beach, Cal.) and Warrant Officer Richard A. Look(CEC, USNR, Iron Mountain, Mich.) Lt. Comdr. W. A. Burke, Jr. (CEC, USNR, Stamford, Conn.) officer-in-charge of the 1006th was aboard the same LST.

Lt. Cmdr., Burke tells the story of the landing.

"Our LST, together with several score others, made up a Task Force, carrying the 46th British Division. The convoy consisted of about over fifty ships and craft, with the 15-inch gun British Monitor *Abercrombie.*

"Around 1600 on 'D minus 1' we sighted the Island of Capri off the Italian Coast. A hostile plane swooped down along the right flank of the convoy and dropped bombs far ahead, getting a YT in the distance. It sent up a tremendous pillar of dark smoke. At about 2000, the British Radio announced the unconditional surrender of the Italian government. Some of the boys were pretty optimistic and thought that the war was over and that next day's landing would be done under a flag of truce. Their optimism was rudely shattered an hour and a half later when we underwent a severe bombing attack from the Luftwaffe.

"On 'D' Day, 9 September 1943, we were up at 0200 to pre-pare the causeways for launching. British destroyers were shelling Red and Green Beaches and adjacent strong points. About 0320, in pitch darkness, the rocket craft let go their bar-rage. As we lay to in the calm water of the bay some four to five miles off the beach, it was a fascinating sight to watch, through field glasses, the terrific discharge of the rocket batteries. They were fired in bunches, enveloping their craft in brilliant sheets of flame, then soaring high up, over and down toward the beach where thunderous explosions took place.

"At 0330—'H' Hour—the first waves of the assault Rangers and Commandos landed in their small craft, to be followed by waves of LCVP, LCI's and LCT's. The theory was that a few hun-dred assault troops should seize the beachhead and squelch enemy resistance prior to the main assault landing of the LST's which would follow at about sunrise. Sometime around 0430, shortly before dawn, four German artillery shells fell in the water close to the causeway. Shrapnel fragments fell over the cause-ways and pounded against the sides of the LST. Twenty-two of our men and Warrant Officer Dick Look were on the causeway, fully exposed to fire, but fortunately no one was hit.

"At 0525 our ship, with causeways rigged for momentum beaching was ordered into Green Beach. We were following the course of the YM [dredger] minesweepers when, about a mile off-shore a large size Italian mine which had been swept to the surface, but not exploded, loomed in the path of the ship. The forward lookout saw the ominous round shape and a frantic ef-fort was made to veer the ship to port, but not enough. The curved end of the inboard causeway hit and rode up over the mine which bounced along under the bottom for about 70 feet before going off against the side of the ship. At the time of the ex-plosion I was sitting on some sand buckets in front of the pilot house. My first blinding impression was of a terrific explosion for-ward. Thinking we had been hit by an aerial bomb, I threw myself to the deck to avoid shrapnel and fragments. There was a blind-ing flame, water towered up, objects were hurled aloft, then a blast of air and a deluge of water and oil fell on us. Luckily, fire did not break out, although how the numerous gasoline tanks of our cargo escaped being ignited will always be a mystery.

The explosion ripped into troop quarters killing and seriously injuring a number of British soldiers.

The ship was still underway, but the causeways were gone and rapidly drifting astern. In the dim light it was possible to see a pontoon or two drifting free, but we did not at first realize that those shadows piled up on the forward weather deck were pontoons blown from the sea. Fortunately, a couple of small craft were in the vicinity which went to the assistance of the Seabees aboard the wrecked causeways. We found out later that there was sufficient warning of the explosion for the men to run to the extreme aft end of the causeway where, although they were violently stunned by the terrific detonation, only two were killed; a big, strapping farm boy from Iowa named Jim Achterhoff, and a chap named Jones who had married the day he came into the Navy. Dick Look's eardrums were punctured, and several others were seriously wounded.

"We did not know whether the ship would stay afloat long enough to reach the beach as she was listing badly. We grounded about 0600, without our causeways, some 250 feet off the shore line with about 11 feet of water at the bow ramp. It was immediately apparent that the beach had not yet been taken. Batteries of 88's and mortars had the range of the beach and kept up the shelling all through 'D' Day. When the extent of the mine damage was finally ascertained, and it was found that the ship would remain afloat, it was decided to retract and attempt to put our combat cargo ashore over one of the other sets of causeways or via LCT's.

"When we were about a half mile off the beach, a British destroyer laid down a smoke screen which protected us from further fire from the shore and enabled us to anchor in the transport area between the Flag Ship Biscayne and the Monitor Abercrombie, transferring our cargo to LCT's."

The second LST to be readied for the run to North Beach was the one on which Lieutenant Harry Stevens, Jr. (CEC, USNR, Salem, Ill.), was officer-in-charge of causeways. The other Seabee officer was Ensign M. T. Jacobs (CEC, USNR, Hopkinsville, Ky.). Jacobs, modest, ruddy-cheeked, a former engineer for the Tennessee Valley Authority, told the story.

"At H-Hour—0330—our LST had moved in to within three miles of the Red section of North Beach," he explained. "We were carrying men of a Hampshire regiment of the 46th British Division. On the tank deck we had six Shermans, with a lot of half-tracks, Bren gun carriers, and ducks. The weather deck was loaded with half-tracks and supply trucks. It was a clear night with a million stars but no moon.

"The 16th Panzers were ready for us. When the small craft began hitting the beach, the Panzers opened up with everything they had. Big guns, 88's and machine guns. Our warships including the cruisers Savannah, Boise and Philadelphia, were with the Southern Attack Force off Paestum, and they returned the fire. The Savannah had pulled in to within a few hundred feet of our LST, and she was blasting with everything she had. German bombers started coming over, so even the guns on the LST's started firing. God, it was hot! And right at that moment we got the order to prepare to launch causeways.

"The Hampshires were about as interested in watching us launch the causeways as in watching all the gunfire. We have those causeways secured by many cables and turn-buckles; and when we prepare to launch, the first thing we have to do is remove all the cables except three. Chopping blocks are rigged under the three remaining cables, and three men stand by with axes waiting for the signal to launch. Can you cut a steel cable with an axe? Sure, when the cable is as taut as those cables are.

"At 0415 we dropped the first causeway, and fifteen minutes later we dropped the second one. All this time we had to shout like hell to one another. The Germans had set one of our tugs afire, so we had a sort of half-light from it. After we drop the causeways, the senior officer and ten men stay on the weather deck of the LST to handle the lines, while the junior officer and twenty-four men get down on the causeways to rig them for the run to the beach.

"We opened the bow doors and let out our duck. We had asked for an hour to rig the causeways, but we had rush orders. Those 175-foot sections are plenty heavy in the water. As junior officer, I had to direct the rigging and ride the causeways. We hitched the duck to one section and began maneuvering it toward the other side of the ship. Shells were popping all around us, but while you are rigging you are so busy you don't mind it so much. It's when you start into the beach and have nothing to do but hold on and pray—that's when you really get scared.

"At 0530 we had finished rigging the causeways into the slide-rule formation alongside the port side of the ship. Mine-sweepers had been working in front of us, so we started our run for the beach. I was lying up at the forward end of the causeway and had plenty of time to look around and see what was going on.

"All twenty-five of us who were lying on the causeways were dressed in two-piece coveralls, helmets and life jackets. We had canteens and 45's on our belts; no other arms. You don't need anybody to tell you to be flat on that causeway, because you feel like the most exposed man in the whole harbor. And that's just what you are. You look at a Stillson wrench lying in front of you, and it looks big enough for you to crawl under it. Honestly, you get the idea that that wrench gives you some protection.

"Off to my left as we were going in, I could see another LST with her set of causeways. That was Lieutenant Commander Burke, our officer-in-charge, with Mitchell and Look. Firing and bombing were going on incessantly. When we were about a mile off the beach, the causeways ridden by Look and his men hit a loose mine, and there was one helluva an explosion. We could see it in the half-light from where we were riding. Their duck, which was running alongside the causeways, was swamped and sunk. The LST, with her bottom stove in, continued but was unable to affect a landing.

"Look and most of his twenty-four men were blown off the causeways by that explosion. It was several days before all of them were located, since they were picked up by various craft. After we saw that explosion, me and my fellows lay on our causeways and prayed for that minesweeper that was going in front of us.

"About 0620—just before sunup—we hit the beach full speed. We cut the causeways loose, but our luck was holding. The beach condition was such that our LST slid right on up to the water's edge, and we didn't need the causeways for her. All we had to do was throw a few sandbags under her ramp and spread the mat. We were held up about ten minutes while the British engineers grabbled landmines, but the Seabees used that ten minutes to good advantage. We had long-handled shovels on the causeways with which to fill sandbags, so we grabbed those shovels and dug slit trenches. Shells were bursting all around us.

"The first vehicle to come off, of course, was our bulldozer. Probably the first American vehicle to land on the continent of Europe was a Seabee bulldozer driven by Raymond J. Calhoun, Machinist's Mate first, of Troy, N.Y. Calhoun came down that ramp, rolled up the beach about fifty feet through the mine markers, then cut to the left right behind a small tractor which had been landed in a small craft by the Commandos. Just at that second the British tractor hit a mine and was blown to hell, killing the driver. Calhoun was blown straight back, head-over, heels, off his bulldozer, and it was a miracle that he didn't break his neck.

"We began unloading our LST and had her unloaded by 0800. We had the causeways standing by, with the duck hitched to the floating end and the bulldozer hitched to the beach end, ready to hook up to any LST that hung short of the beach. But three more LST's came in, and all of them made it clear to the shore line. That was the best beach we'll ever see for LST operations.

"The Hampshires had pushed on in and were tangling with the 16th Panzers. Shellfire from 88's was still bothering us on the beach. About 1000, I witnessed the goriest sight of the war for me. Seven or eight Hampshires decided that they'd brew up a spot of tea on the beach. They built a fire and had the water boiling when one of them called to me: 'Say, chappie, come and have a spot o' tea.' I started walking toward them and was within fifty feet of them when a landmine went off right under that fire. The explosion knocked me flat, and when I got up every damn one of those Hampshires was dead and mangled.

"Three of our causeway platoons had reached Red Beach by 0700. Only Mitchell's platoon, which had hit the mine, had been turned back. The LST that McGrath and Butterfield came in with was hit eleven times on the run-in, and one shell hit her elevators so that nothing could be unloaded off of her weather deck. They unloaded her tank deck; then she retracted.

"Late that afternoon, our men established a bivouac about 300 yards from where we had landed. We stayed there on the beach for ten days during which the bombing, shelling and fighting continued almost constantly. The crisis was on the fifth and sixth days, when it appeared that perhaps we were going to have to pull a Dunkirk, but those Britishers finally turned the tide. We Seabees had no further casualties on the beach, but we had some close calls.

"Red Woodmancy (Charles W. Woodmancy, Carpenter's Mate second, Mirror Lake, N.H.), who had won the Legion of Merit in Sicily, refused to dig himself a slit trench. He boasted that he could sleep through any barrage the Germans could lay down. He had set up a cot with a mosquito netting over it. One night he slept through an air raid, and next morning he found that a bomb fragment had come inside his mosquito netting and broken the frame of his cot without waking him up.

"We had all sorts of fellows in our gang. Bob Russell (Robert G. Russell, Shipfitter second, Lynn, Mass.) was a Boston blueblood. He was close to fifty; he had finished in the same Harvard class as Governor Saltonstall. He was cynical as hell; kept us amused with card tricks; and had been awarded the Purple Heart after he had been wounded in a torpedoing before Sicily. Russell walked up on the beach and looked at young Achterhoff's body which we had found and laid out.

"There's life for you," he commented. "A fine young lad like that gets knocked off on the run-in. Yet a worthless old squirt like me—hell, the Germans can torpedo me, bomb me, shell me and grenade me in two goddam wars and they can't kill me for hell. Justice, huh!"

Lieutenant George H. Shanahan (CEC, USNR, Alton, Illinois) and Lieutenant (jg) W. C. Ginner (CEC, USNR, Berkeley, Cal.) were in charge of Platoon "H." Their LST anchored off Red Beach Wednesday night, 8 September. At 0430 the next morning the causeways were dropped and rigged and ready for the run-in. Lieutenant Shanahan reported:

"Flames from German planes had lighted up the sky like daylight, so it was easy to see to work although we were a little uneasy. On the way in we received word that the causeways were not needed, and the men were brought back aboard. Our ship was hit eight times by German 88's from shore batteries and seven of our men were injured. When the ship beached we cast off the causeways, anchored them, and unloaded all our gear and equipment.

"We spent the next few days helping to clear traffic and build some roadways. An air raid or two a day kept us on our toes. One evening at twilight, I went over to Lieutenant Zak's bunk and we were talking when the air raid siren sounded. A few 88's whined over us. Zak and I hit his foxhole at the same time and we were really wedged in. After a short time, something hit the ground about five feet away with a thud. Zak and I hugged the ground a little closer and waited for the explosion. Nothing happened. After an eternity had passed, Lieutenant Ginner stuck his head out of his foxhole and said: 'Jesus, it's a bomb!' We got away from there quick. Later we found out that it was an empty metal container which carries about a dozen personnel bombs."

Platoon "E" was led by Lieutenant Alexander M. Zak (CEC, USNR, Franklin, N.H.) and Lieutenant (jg) Fred W. Gensch (CEC, USNR, Elizabethtown, Ky.). Lieutenant Zak's story follows:

"We started our run for the beach at 0655 and were proceeding at a good speed when German 88's began to fly all around us. Ten men were on the causeway to handle the deck lines. An 88-shell burst on the causeway and caught three of the men. A second shell got three more. The 88's followed us all the way in but didn't hit us again. Getting the wounded off the causeway was the next problem. We lowered a wire basket stretcher and removed one man. Murphy, our platoon chief on the causeway, was seriously wounded in the chest by shell fragments but he waved the corpsmen away, insisting that some of the other wounded be taken off first. He died a few days later after being evacuated by a British hospital ship.

"Machine gun bullets were bouncing all around us. There was absolutely no protection for the men on the causeway except to lie flat on the deck. We finally beached in six feet of water about 30 feet from shore. With the aid of an abandoned bulldozer on the beach we were able to maneuver the causeway almost parallel to the beach, yet near enough to the LST so that its ramp rested on the causeway. A couple of hours later we had completed the unloading of our equipment."

"We launched our causeways just before daylight," Wallace explained, "and we began our first run toward Green Beach about 0730. But we were turned back. The fire was too heavy. The Royal Stud Farm was located on our beach. The land rolled upward in terrace back from the beach. There was an old concrete silo which the Germans used for observation. The 16th Panzers had emplaced their tanks and 88's behind stone wall and all through those terraces.

"The advance platoons of the Hampshires had landed in small boats before daylight, and they were up there in those pastures fighting the tanks with rifles and grenades. We had to get in there with some heavy stuff to help them. But it was 1230 before we finally got up to the beach. It took runs to make it."

"And those three runs were not as easy as they sound," Cantey put in. "Me and twenty-four men were lying on those causeways for six hours in broad daylight. And bombs and shells were dropping around us the whole time. On the first run-in, a tug was hit within a hundred feet of us, and the tug ran on in and hit a mine. On the second run-in, some of our boys jumped off in the water and trailed themselves behind the causeways to try to get some cover.

"When we got to the beach, all we could do was dig slit trenches in front of that stone wall and get in them. The Hampshires had pushed on up in the pastures, trying to knock out the tanks, but there was a dead Hampshire every ten foot. Some mistake had been made, and we weren't supposed to have landed there, so all we could do was hang on and wait. That night about 2300 the Hampshires got orders to fall back to the beach, so that our cruisers could lay down a barrage on the tank positions. The barrage started about 0130 and lasted an hour.

"The cruisers knocked out a lot of tanks, and next day we were able to unload. The Hampshires punched in about 400 yards. During the night a German shell came through the wall and passed about six inches over Frank Wilson. Wilson looked at the hole and wasn't scared a bit—then. But the next morning he started shaking, and I'll be damned if he didn't shake for ten days.

"After we had unloaded our LST," Wallace added, "there was little else for us to do but wait. No more LST's would come into Green Beach because the going was so hot. It was touch-and-go there for six days. The Hampshires just had to tangle with those tanks with grenades and Molotov cocktails. We helped the Hampshires with their supplies and with their dead. They had a thousand men killed there around the Stud Farm.

"The strangest thing about that fight was the way those blooded cattle and horses died. The cattle were pure white, and I think they were just scared to death. I saw scores of them, bloated, with all four feet sticking straight in the air, but there wasn't a mark on them. Concussion from naval shells may have killed some of them, but the rest must have died from sheer fear. We buried them with the bulldozer.

"Unkenholtz was an even bigger problem than he had been in Sicily. He had helped build New York subways and was brave as a pack of wildcats. But he looked more German than any German I ever saw. So, no matter how heavy the shelling got, I had to order him to wear his chief's cap instead of his helmet. Let him put on a helmet and he looked so much like a German paratrooper that the Hampshires would have shot him. To make matters worse, he was always sneaking up to the front, since his chief ambition was to capture one of his cousins. He has six first cousins in the German Army.

"About the eighth day, when the Hampshires were able to push on in, we got in on some choice souvenir-hunting. If we could get to those German tanks before they burned up, we could get radios, wristwatches and American 45's. All the tank crews in the 16th Panzers seemed to have English tommy guns, American 45's and English 'compo' rations. That 'compo' ration is the best in the world, and the Germans captured enough of them at Tobruk to feed the 16th Panzers for a year.

"On the tenth day the situation had eased to where we could join the other Seabee platoons on Red Beach."

As previously explained, the entire operation on South Beach was an American show. Units of the 36th American Division had begun landing on South Beach about 0330, the same time as the British began landing on North Beach. But the 36th met unexpected resistance. The two Italian divisions which had been guarding that sector had been replaced by two crack German divisions. Except that the Germans had fewer tanks, the resistance on South Beach was just as fierce as that on North Beach.

Senior Civil Engineer Corps officer in charge of causeways for the South Beach landing was Lieutenant C. H. "Buck" Buchanan (CEC, USNR, Washington, D.C). His deck officer on causeways was Warrant Officer Francis L. Collins (CEC, USNR, Fall River, Mass.).

"Our LST was loaded with a tank detachment of the 36th Division," Buchanan recalled.

"About 0400 we had moved into the bay to a position about three miles off the Blue section of South Beach. We had our traditional battle breakfast, which is supposed to be beefsteak and fried eggs, but which is never anything but Spam and powdered eggs. We could see the shells bursting over on the beach, and we knew the Texas boys needed their tanks; but we didn't get orders to launch causeways until 0630.

"Our platoon always drops both causeways at the same time. It makes a bigger splash, which entertains the soldiers. We were rigged and ready to run for the beach at 0715, but we couldn't get in. The artillery fire was too heavy. We put out our smoke pots for cover and inched in, but the minesweepers were having a bad time trying to clear us a channel. Collins was determined to stand up on the causeways, and I finally had to order him down.

"When we passed LST 309, Collins was standing up, so one of the boys on 309 yelled: 'Say, Collins, pay me that five bucks before you go in. If I don't get it now, I never will!' The boys had been on the causeways for six hours when we finally squared off behind two minesweepers and began the run for the beach. The fire was hot; one shell swept our captain's cabin clean off; but we pushed in to within 300 feet of the water's edge where we grounded hard. We had manipulated the causeways perfectly, however, for they ran clear on up on dry land, and we were connected and unloading ten minutes later.

"Our beachhead was about twenty-five yards deep at that time. We unloaded the tanks and they went charging on up past our front to attack the German strong points. Old General Lange was sure glad to see us. He had tears in his eyes when I met him. 'I just knew you boys would come in,' he said. He seemed so glad to see us that I loaned him my jeep.

"Our causeways acted as a magnet for LST's, so we did nothing but unload ships for the next twenty-four hours. We did dig some slit trenches, but we dug them too deep, and we found them full of salt water the first time we jumped into them. Olson's platoon was working around on Green Beach, and Sanders' platoon was working on Red Beach.

"At exactly 1010 the next morning—D-Day plus one—I heard a heavy shell explode up in Olson's direction. I looked at my watch because I had a feeling that that shell had killed some of our men. I ran up there and found that Olson's whole platoon had been shattered by the bomb burst. Olson, Shuttlesworth and Huss were dead, and several others were badly injured. Since all of the LST's on South Beach had to be unloaded over causeways, I reorganized the platoon and we went back to work. In spite of the bomb hit, that platoon unloaded ten ships that day.

"Sanders' platoon suffered a bomb hit on the same day. Two men were killed and several injured, but the platoon worked steadily rolling the stuff ashore. We unloaded a total of 190 LST's over the causeways on South Beach before we were able to move into Naples harbor and begin using piers and Liberty ships.

"The 1006th Pontoon Detachment of twenty-eight officers and 300 men suffered 23 per cent casualties. One officer and seven men were killed, and nine officers and fifty-seven men were awarded the Purple Heart."

The adventures of the 1006th Detachment began on the night of June 21, 1943, when a convoy carrying pontoons was attacked off the Algerian coast. The convoy was churning through a calm sea when, without warning, torpedoes crashed into the two LST's. Both ships were piled high with pontoon gear. The Germans apparently had realized the importance of pontoon gear to our planned operations, and they were trying to prevent its future use as planned.

Warrant Officer George Bethune and a group of Seabees from both the 1006th Detachment and the 70th Battalion were standing near the stern of one of the LST's on the ship's weather deck.

"The torpedo struck right under the stern," he reported. "We caught it full force. The next thing I knew I was in the water. My ankle was numb, and there was a terrific pain in my back. I heard a man screaming, so I swam about fifty yards over to him. He was about to drown, so I slipped out of my life jacket and put it under him. I am a very strong swimmer, having kicked around in North Carolina streams all my life.

"I noticed another man floundering in the water. I swam to him, pulled him over to the first man, and tied them both to my life jacket. Then I swam to an LCT and directed the craft to the two men. We hauled them out, but one of them died of his injuries."

Six Seabees were killed by the torpedoes. They were Walter J. Burroughs, Carpenter's Mate second, Corfu, N.Y.; Algert J. Goba, Seaman first, Norwood, Mass.; Ross L. Toler, Electrician's Mate second, Pittsburgh, Pa.; Armandzor P. Vanasse, Seaman first, East Hampton, Mass.; Thomas M. Vargoshe, Carpenter's Mate first, Bridgeport, Conn.; and Charlie R. Walton, Water tender second, Memphis, Tenn.

Many more Seabees would have died from injuries had it not been for the heroic work of Lieutenant Irving Silverman (Medical Corps, USNR, Worcester, Mass.). Doctor Silverman was the only medical officer in the convoy when the torpedo struck. Most of the hospital corpsmen on the LST were among the wounded. Working steadily for more than twenty-four hours, much of the time in complete darkness with only a flashlight to guide him, Doctor Silverman handled 72 cases, administered plasma, and performed 11 operations. He then supervised the transfer of the 56 most badly wounded men to a rescue vessel.

The 1006th handled all the causeways and LST unloading in the American portion of the Sicilian operation. The causeway platoons worked under tremendous difficulties caused by both the flat beach condition and the high winds. When the invasion fleet arrived off the Sicilian coast at 0200 on July 10, 1943, a five-foot surf was running around both Gela and Licata. The Germans were confident that we would not attempt to land; and, indeed, the decision as to whether to land or not hung in the balance several hours.

Buck Buchanan's experience on the flagship LST 389 is noteworthy, if not truly typical.

"That damn 389 is a hard-luck ship." Buchanan said. "When she was leaving her U.S. port she got tangled up in the minefield and was stranded there for three days while somebody figured a way to get her out. Going into Sicily everything went wrong. First, we had to open the bow doors and letdown the ramp in order to let the duck out. The high waves picked up the ramp and dropped it so hard that the ramp chains broke. We couldn't close the bow doors. We headed into the storm with the bow doors open and took so much water that the whole goddamn tank deck was two-feet deep in water.

"We had no way to pump the water off the tank deck, so we shifted ballast and threw a whole wall of water over every man on the tank deck. Then we broke the elevator winch, and thus had no winch for our haul-back line on the causeways. When we finally laid the causeways against the beach, we had to man the haul-back line with soldiers. We finally got to the beach about 1800 on D-Day, then had to retract and run back out, leaving

Collins and the men ashore, all of them wet as hell and with nothing to eat. We tried to send dry clothes into them, but somebody had set the small boat adrift. Collins and his boys stole some Italian uniforms to keep warm, and we took them for Italian prisoners when we ran back in the next morning. After that we got going and unloaded a lot of ships, but the first twenty-four hours was disheartening as hell."

All the leading LST's, which had to carry the causeways, had trouble lowering their ramps in the high waves. The moment the ponderous ramp was lowered into the water to let out an amphibious truck, the fierce waves would toss the ramp up, then drop it, breaking the retaining chains. Then the bow doors couldn't be closed, and if the ship attempted to make way against the sea, the tank deck was flooded. Some of the LST's solved this problem by backing into the beach; others were taken in tow by LCT's.

"We had some crazy experiences on that beach at Sicily," Mr. Canty recalled. "One LST came up to our causeway with a load of Arab donkeys on its weather deck. The dogfaces had painted chevrons on the donkeys, making top sergeants out of most of them. We had to bring those donkeys down the elevators and walk them across the causeways.

"Another LST had a load of African Spahis aboard. The damn Spahis came across the causeways riding their horses, wearing their red caps, waving their sabers, and yelling like hell.

"The Italian prisoners were both funny and helpful. Unloading ammunition, we would use amphibious trucks, which don't need the causeways. They can just run right out in the water to an LST, climb inside her, then run out with a load of ammunition and deliver it to the troops in the field. These ducks would take a load of ammunition to the troops and bring back a load of Italian prisoners, riding on top of the duck.

"Apparently the Italians had never seen a duck. When the duck on which they were riding would head suddenly out into the water, all the Italians would jump up and cross themselves; then sit down, stoically expecting the worst.

"The Seabees are the middlemen of the souvenir business. The paratroops and assault troops go in and get first pickings; then they bring the loot down to the beach and sell it to the Seabees; then the Seabees sell it to the ships' crews. Italian carbines and German Iron Crosses brought the highest prices in Sicily.

"One of the best deals we made, however, was in trading a pig to an LST crew for three dozen eggs and some canned goods. O'Neill and Goempel [Author Note: "These two were a pair of characters. O'Neill (Chief Boatswain's Mate William J. O'Neill, Cape May Court House, N.J.) is six feet two; Goempel (Jacob G. Goempel, Carpenter's Mate second) is five three. Goempel wears a No. 3 shoe, so small that the Navy couldn't fit him, and he had to wear sneakers on his first liberty. He claims the smallest foot of the Second World War."] came leading the squealing pig back one night. They were going to butcher it, but they decided that the weather wasn't quite right. The pig kept squealing, so next day they traded it to the LST skipper. A week later that LST pulled up to the causeway again, and we could hear that pig squealing. The skipper gave us another three dozen eggs to take the pig off his hands. We then had ham and eggs for four days."

During twenty-three days of round-the-clock work in Sicily, the Seabees unloaded 10,000 vehicles from LST's over the causeways.

Seabees confab during Operation Stalemate
(Peleliu, November 1944.)

9: We Build Two Atlantic Roads

THE SEABEES WHO HAVE TOILED ALONG THE North and South Atlantic roads may deserve more credit for their work than their fellows who happened to be assigned to the more active war zones. Most men who have to go to war prefer active war theaters; they'll choose bombs to boredom every time. It's easy for Americans to perform prodigious feats of construction under fire; what isn't so easy is to stick to the long, difficult job when the weather is muggy, the food is lousy, the equipment doesn't arrive, and the only enemies for you to fight are the insects.

When this war is finished I hope someone will devise a medal with a lot of gold on it: a medal suitable for those members of the Army and Navy who "fought" the war in the lonely, uncomfortable places of the world; who never heard a shot fired; who never saw a cameraman or a newspaperman; who never once marched in a parade; who cussed and groused and griped; but who, somehow, were able to generate enough motivation within themselves to get the job done. A lot of Seabees who worked at places like Freetown, West Africa, or the Galapagos Islands will qualify for this medal.

In August 1942, forty Seabees arrived at Kissy Flats, near Freetown. They called themselves the "Dirty Forty," and they were the forerunners of the 65th Battalion, the first Seabee battalion to serve on the other side of the Atlantic. The temperature was 140 degrees. Ten-foot-long snakes were as plentiful as earthworms around a pigpen. Some docks had to be built. The Dirty Forty had been rushed in to take over; to repair the rusting machinery; to get the job going again. New equipment was "on the way," but the Dirty Forty had no fancy illusions as to when it might arrive. There were a lot of submarines between them and America.

Give a Seabee a pair of pliers and a roll of baling wire, and there is almost nothing he can't do with it. The Dirty Forty repaired some steam shovels and started tearing up the face of Africa. To keep the natives from standing around in the way, they put the natives to work hewing gumwood piles. The piles were fifty to eighty feet long. The harbor bottom was of hard volcanic lava, so hard that the piles had to be iron-capped before they could be driven.

The old piledriver at Freetown was powered by steam and designed to work from the shore. The Dirty Forty converted it from steam to compressed air power. They mounted it on a barge.

When one of its motors expired, the Seabees took a truck engine, rigged it up with a chain drive taken from a decrepit steamroller, and had that piledriver driving like hell out in the middle of the harbor.

The British were amazed. Forty Americans had turned Freetown upside down. They had all the ancient machinery coughing away; natives were scampering around with undreamed of energy; and a few of the natives were even operating machines.

The Dirty Forty and the other detachments which arrived to help make up the 65th Battalion worked around the clock seven days a week. For recreation, the men fished and explored with the natives. The West African natives are funnier and more interesting than the natives in the South Pacific.

The men of the 65th found native undertakers a constant source of amusement. Competition among them is as fierce as among their American counterparts. One ingenious fellow enjoyed a temporary business boom when he installed a bar in his "parlors," but a competitor retaliated—apparently with American connivance—by offering free American cigarettes with each of his funerals.

Cigarettes prove powerful incentives to native effort. And the makers of Kools may have this advertising tip free from the Seabees. One day a member of the Dirty Forty handed a native a Kool, the cigarette with menthol in it. The native took a puff, rolled his eyes as though he had been bewitched, then grinned: "Good! Good! Make you feel good!" That night the tom-toms were beating, telling the news of the new cigarette, and next day 500 natives were clamoring for work and the new cigarette. Many pilings were hewed that week for Kools.

David M. Belasco, Shipfitter third, Redwood City, Cal., joined a native tribe. Instead of a tattoo on his chest, he wears an acid brand put there by a native girl. All the men were offered wives for ten dollars; but one of the men was offered a special bargain.

One old chief tried to sell a daughter for eight dollars. When refused, he offered his son's wife; and when she was turned down he tried like hell to sell his own wife!

The operations in North Africa were a British and United States Army show, but three Seabee battalions built the installations for our Navy. These battalions were the 54th, led by Commander Wallace L. Rinehart (CEC, USNR, Webster Groves, Mo.); the 70th, led by Commander Arthur J. Benline (CEC, USNR, Bronx, N.Y.); and the 120th, led by Commander George A. Rezac (CEC, USNR, Hiwassee Dam, N.C.). The 54th landed at Arzew, Algeria, with the invasion convoy, while the 70th landed at Casablanca. The 120th later moved into Arzew.

The 54th is distinguished by the four Fieger brothers. These brothers, Canadian-born of Russian extraction, are all of Los Angeles and all are shipfitters. They form a family gun crew for the battalion, manning twin .50-caliber anti-aircraft guns. They are Francis J. Fieger, 19; Lawrence A. Fieger, 24; Anthony L. Fieger, 27; and John A. Fieger, Jr., 28.

The 120th has made an earth-shaking discovery which may cause a mass migration to Africa when the war is over. It seems that there is a combination of wind and sun at Arzew which restores life to dead scalps and causes luxuriant growths of new hair.

"European princes suffering from baldness in youth," writes a 120th correspondent, "came to the blue sea to the south where the balmy sea breezes and medicinal sunshine restored life to the dead cells and produced new hair. The sun here is also supposed to diminish and eventually erase all trace of freckles. With regard to the latter we have no positive proof, but with regard to the former it is a known fact that some of the Seabees of this battalion were as bald as any billiard ball when they came to Africa and they are now sporting a new crop of hair. Others have noticed that they have more hair, while still others have remarked on rapid hair growth."

This report, circulated widely among the Seabees, has brought an insistent demand that all bald Seabees be placed in one battalion, and that the "Bald Battalion" be assigned one year's duty at Arzew.

On the North Atlantic highway, the 17th, 64th and 69th Battalions have built the base at Argentia, Newfoundland; the Ninth and 28th Battalions are responsible for the vast Navy installations in Iceland.

In the Caribbean and South Atlantic, the 31st and 49th Battalions drew the assignment to Bermuda, but there was working to do even in that technicolored area. Damaged ships had to be repaired; cargo had to be restored in vessels buffeted by heavy weather; and always there is the job of more fuel storage, more wharves, more drydocks.

The 30th, 80th and 83rd Battalions built the extensive base at Trinidad, while the 1012th Detachment drew the lonely assignment on the Galapagos Islands, which belong to Ecuador and which guard the Pacific approaches to the Panama Canal. The 1012th did previous chores in the Canal Zone, Nicaragua and Honduras.

10: The Northern Highway to Victory

TO COMPREHEND THE MAGNITUDE OF AMERICAN war enterprise in the Pacific; to understand how this war is as much a war of highways as were the wars of the Romans, one needs to travel in slow stages the 2000-mile arc from Seattle to Attu. When you have studied this military highroad, you can realize how vast a construction job we have undertaken. No other nation in history has or could have performed such feats. Only a nation with our industrial might and with our men who know how to use our machines could have projected its industrial strength so far, so powerfully, and in so many directions.

The road to Attu is only one of five great roads we are building—two others are in the Pacific and two in the Atlantic. Yet I think the road to Attu is the most impressive one of all, because most of it was built across islands which were bare and practically uninhabited before our road-builders arrived. In the Atlantic the islands were inhabited and partially developed. The same was true to a lesser degree in the Central and South Pacific. But the Aleutians were nothing but bare, tundra-covered, volcanic mountaintops jutting up out of a thousand fathoms of ice water. They supported no animal life; there wasn't a tree or a shrub west of Dutch Harbor.

The Aleutian Islands are a prehistoric connecting link between two land masses which modern man was willing to ignore as worthless until the Japs launched their war against us.

Methodically, I traveled the Seattle-Attu road in the summer of 1943. A traveling companion during much of the trip was Father Bernard Hubbard, the "Glacier Priest," whose twenty years of devotion to Alaska and the Aleutians have paid rich dividends to both our Army and Navy. Aboard ship, Father Hubbard spent his morning lecturing to the men and his afternoons lecturing to the officers, enthusiastically sharing his knowledge of the country which he knows so well.

The first stop after leaving Seattle is Sitka, where Seabee stevedores swarm over the ship to unload mail and supplies. Sitka looks like Jack London's Alaska: high, snow-capped mountains and dense forests, totem poles and a weather-beaten Russian church. The war came to Sitka long ago and brought the new docks, great warehouses, hangars and runways; then the war moved on, leaving only maintenance crews, patrol pilots and sentinels. The 22nd Battalion and a detachment of the 45th did the Navy work at Sitka.

Four hundred miles to the north and west, at Kodiak, you reach an island which, unbelievably, was once an "advance base." We had hardly begun its development when the Japs struck. Radio Tokyo announced its capture by Jap troops in November 1942. But the Seabees had arrived with their portable sawmills; with all the mighty machines with which America was built; and they converted it into a sea and air fortress many times as strong as Singapore ever was.

I sat in a petty officers' club, drank beer and swapped yarns with Buck Buckholts, of Flushing, N.Y.; with P. J. Blanchard, of Spokane, Wash.; and with Lloyd Allen, of Hanford, Cal.—all chief petty officers of the 43rd Battalion.

Around midnight, Lloyd Allen, who owns a farm and a restaurant down in the San Joaquin Valley and is thus a chief commissary steward, took us up on a hill to his mess hall where his cooks were rolling biscuit and baking cakes for the next day. He performed some magic with hamburger and onions, and we drank more beer and ate and looked out over the great base.

"I guess the war seems farther from here than it does from home?" he asked. I nodded. San Francisco and New York had blackouts; Kodiak didn't.

The array of battalions which worked at Kodiak measures its magnitude. The 12th Battalion pioneered there; then came part of the 23rd, the 38th, the 41st, the 43rd, and the 45th. That many Seabee battalions can move a lot of dirt, and in this war, victory seems to favor the side which can move the most dirt.

Four hundred miles west of Kodiak is Dutch Harbor. Dutch Harbor is farther west than Pearl Harbor. Long after the Pearl Harbor disaster, Dutch Harbor was our most advanced base in the Pacific. Jap bombers attacked it once but never returned. The Fourth Seabee Battalion was rushed in there in the spring of 1942—the same time that the First, Second and Third were being rushed to the South Pacific. The Fourth was reinforced at Dutch by the Eighth, the 12th, the 13th, the 21st, a detachment of the 23rd, the 51st, and the 52nd. Some of these battalions later moved westward, but all of them helped to give Dutch its mighty guns, its acres of tank farm, its catacombs of torpedoes and bombs, its runways, hangars, warehouses and miles of barracks.

West of Dutch is Umnak, with airstrips and barracks, and west of Umnak is Adak. Both Boulder Dam and the Pyramids could have been built with the labor that was expended on Adak. It's a large island, once completely bare and uninhabited. Then the Army Engineers and the Seabees arrived. Hundreds of trucks now roar over its highways. Many thousands of men now live in its barracks, Quonset huts, Pacific huts and "winterized" tents. There is regular bus service between its various service communities. There are steam baths, ballparks, beer halls, capacious theaters, a hundred great warehouses, several big piers. Its hills are crammed with torpedoes, bombs and shells; small-arms ammunition dumps are everywhere. There are Army hospitals, Navy hospitals, a cemetery, newspapers, and a radio broadcasting station which sends out the constant reminder that this is the Northern Highway to Victory

The 32nd Battalion pioneered at Adak. Then came the 12th, pushing on from Dutch; detachments of the 23rd, 21st and 45th; and the 22nd, 38th, 42nd, 52nd, and Fifth Specials (Stevedores). To provide acres of smooth surface for their warehouses, one battalion simply moved a range of hills into the sea.

West—always the movement is westward—of Adak is Amchitka and a repetition of the story. Once bare tundra; then the Engineers and the Seabees; now docks, warehouses, roads, tank farms, huts and the finest airstrip in the Aleutians. Detachments of the 23rd and 42nd Battalions did the Navy work at Amchitka. West of Amchitka is Kiska, then Attu; and already Attu is another Adak. Detachments of the 12th and 23rd Battalions landed with the Army at Attu; they were followed by the 22nd.

The Jap islands jutting out toward the Aleutians are the Kuriles; and Paramushiro, the advance Jap base in the Kuriles, is 700 miles from Attu. It's 1,200 miles from Paramushiro to Tokyo.

Notice those giant steps: Seattle to Sitka to Kodiak to Dutch Harbor to Adak to Amchitka to Attu to Paramushiro. These are steps which the Japs planned to take in reverse. They had expected to bomb our great shipyards and aircraft plants at Seattle and Portland from bases in Alaska. We tinned their own plans against them because we could move and build faster than they could.

But notice those steps again. It took us two years to build that road. True, the weather opposition was fierce; but there was little Jap opposition. The nearer we get to Tokyo, the tougher the going will be; the longer the distances will become; and this spells time and more time. Those steps explain the nature of our war with Japan. Always we must clear new road of the enemy; then we must construct our bases; then, and only then, can we wind up and sock again.

It's the long, slow process of projecting our industrial might. Completed, these military roads are wide, strong and well protected. P-38's can leave a California factory one day and be in action over Paramushiro the next day. B-17's can take off from Seattle in the morning and bomb Paramushiro that night. Great merchant fleets can ply the road in safety. But this is only because the road has been built. Now the war can move over this road at the speed of a P-38; but the road had to be built at the speed of a Seabee on a bulldozer.

General MacArthur has said that this war is a business of, "advancing the bomber lines." The Seabees are the world's fastest advancers of bomber lines, but even for them the process takes time.

When our forces made the dry-run into Kiska, I landed with a detachment of the 38th Seabee Battalion which had orders to get heavy equipment ashore and build a small operations base as quickly as possible. We landed in an area where 10,000 Japs had lived and worked for a year, so I was able to compare Seabee work with Jap work. I wanted to find the explanation of the Seabees; I wanted to know why and how they perform their miracles.

I found many clues aboard ship before the landing. The first clue was the ship herself and the way she was loaded. She was designed to carry 300 Seabees and all the equipment and supplies they would need for several weeks of intensive operations. She had been loaded to "unravel;" high on top of her deck cargo were the two pontoon barges which would hit the water first; next was a bulldozer which would start clearing a road from the beach; next was a crane which would sit on one of the barges and unload the other; next were the Athey wagons which had tractor treads and which could carry the supplies off the beach; and so on down to the last piece of lumber in the bottom of a hold.

There would be no plumbers on Kiska who would have to wait for their tools; the tools would unravel as needed. The bitter days when Seabees lacked equipment were past; this was August 1943.

The next clue was in the officers and men. Commander Lawrence A. Cline (CEC, USNR, Los Angeles, Cal.) was a firm-jawed, affable veteran of thirty years in the construction business. All of his officers and chief petty officers were men of wide experience, proved specialists in various types of construction. Some of them had owned their own businesses; others had been superintendents on big projects like Grand Coulee Dam. As we neared Kiska, conferences were being held all over the ship. The draftsmen were in one hold completing the blueprints; the electricians were in another studying their plans; the cargo-handlers were preparing to launch their barges; the earth-movers were discussing terrain; the mechanics were checking up on the heavy equipment.

And the men? Were they the unskilled, uneducated type commonly supposed to make up 'labor battalions'? Far from it. There was not one unskilled, inexperienced man in the entire detachment. The men had been chosen on the basis of their civilian experience and skill. There was no place on that ship for the man who didn't know his trade.

At the order to begin unloading, every man was at his post. The pontoon barges hit the water. A heavy crane was swung down to one of the barges, lashed to it, and the barge headed for the beach. The barge was driven hard up on the beach, and the crane was in position to unload all cargo brought alongside. Bulldozers and tractor wagons went on the second barge. On the beach, men began laying the steel mat across the soft sand so that trucks could roll off and disperse the supplies.

The major landing problem at Kiska, as on all the Aleutian Islands, was tundra. This watery mass of grass and mud lies six to thirty inches deep on top of sand and volcanic rock. No rubber-tired truck can move in it. So, the first task is to get some sort of road on which the trucks can move the supplies away from the beach and disperse them against the constant threat of enemy bombing.

There are two ways of handling tundra. The best way is to blade it off completely, run ditches, then add gravel to the sand, and you have a permanent road which holds up even under winter snows. We have built miles of such roads in the Aleutians. The quicker way is to spread a layer of rock on top of the tundra and let the traffic mash the rock into the wiry mass.

At Kiska, the Japs had provided some temporary roads. Working laboriously for a year with hand picks, hand shovels and light trucks, they had built twenty-six miles of roads leading from the beach to their gun emplacements, supply dumps, airstrip and living quarters. This Jap work cut many days off our occupation schedule, but the Jap roads were not built for American rolling stock. They were thin, one-way strips of rock laid atop the tundra, and these strips simply disappeared into the mud when our heavy machines rolled over them. We had to have more rock, and quickly.

The 38th had anticipated this difficulty. The hill where the Japs got their rock was within 300 yards of the beach, and miners with air drills and dynamite were among the first Seabees to hit the beach. Before night the electricians had turned floodlights against the hill face, and all night long the drills sputtered angrily. Blasts shook the island, and by morning a dragline had been hauled up and was enacting the familiar American scene of scooping up ravenous mouthfuls of rock and spitting it into dump trucks.

At the end of a week, the 38th had moved thousands of yards of rock out of that hillside, reinforced all the Jap roads in our area and widened them to two-way, and jeep, truck, halftrack and bulldozer traffic had become so heavy on Kiska that the SP's had to begin directing it. In one week about fifty Seabees with their machines had moved as much rock as hundreds of Japs had moved in one year.

Men and machines were the explanation. J. W. "Hooligan" Maxwell, the heavy-fisted, six-foot-two machinist's mate who directed the dynamiting of that hill, had spent twenty-two years in the mills around Carlsbad, N.M. The man operating the dragline was a veteran of many years with Henry Kaiser. Everybody was handling familiar tools.

The most helpful favor the Japs did us was to leave their communication lines almost intact. There being no trees in the

Aleutians, the Japs had brought creosoted poles all the way from Japan and had strung many miles of line. Chief Electrician's Mate Charlie Pankonin of Chicago and his gang only had to reset a few of the poles, attach our portable generators and turn on the lights and power.

"Damn nice of the Japs to save us so much work," Pankonin remarked. "This is easier than my old job of keeping the lights on in Lincoln Park."

Jap living methods set us to holding our noses both literally and figuratively. If you can imagine dead, decaying rats under a pigpen floor which has been sprinkled with sickeningly sweet powder you are getting close to the odor of a deserted Jap house. The Japs sleep shoulder to shoulder in sleeping bags which lie flat on a platform about a foot off the ground. Except for this platform, the houses have dirt floors, and the little rats don't bother to brave the Aleutian winds to make their toilets. What few heads—Navy for latrine—they had built were nothing but shallow holes just outside their huts.

On the tenth day after our landing we had a head in a Quonset hut, complete with Mr. Crane's best toilet fixtures, concrete floor, automatic hot water boiler, showers and General Electric's best washing machines. Our plumbers had kept pace with the electricians and roadbuilders.

The only Jap building with a concrete floor and sink was their galley, and we quickly pressed it into service as a photo lab. It was about 12 x 24 feet, with big pots set into a coal-burning oven, and it was completely surrounded by a tundra revetment. Harold Lee Reed Cooper, of Freeport, N.Y., the battalion photographer, searched the place for booby traps, then began shamefully using promises of photographs to bribe the electricians into running a line and the plumbers into sticking a plug into a waterline for him. He used a 30-foot piece of Jap hose to bring the water from the line over the revetment and into the galley. He then hung a tarpaulin around his sink for a dark room and was ready for business.

Radio Tokyo makes much noise about the "barbarous American souvenir hunters." They shouldn't call us barbarous; but from top-ranking officers down to the lowest seaman second, the Seabees are avid collectors of Jap junk. By the end of the first week we would have had to charter a special ship to move all the ashtrays, belt buckles and knives which the machinists had made from fittings from a two-man Jap sub; together with the usual complement of opium pipes, grenades, knee-mortar shells, rabbit-fur lined helmets and so on.

However, by far the greatest curiosity on Kiska was not anything the Japs had left, but an exotic gadget which somehow turned up in our equipment. I was passing the "plumbing shop" on the sixth day when I saw a curious cluster of soldiers and Seabees examining the strange object.

"Say, mate," one of them yelled to me, "come here and tell us what this damn thing is." They had thought they were uncrating a regulation Crane commode, but this apparatus didn't seem to be built right.

I looked at it and couldn't have been more astonished had it been a camel from the Sahara Desert. The damn thing was a bidet! With a few illustrations I managed to explain its workings to these incredulous and amazed construction men, but no one could explain how it got there. We finally had to hide it to prevent loss of man-hours to the war effort.

The apparatus was really an insult to the fierceness of the Seabees, particularly since they are the only service organization which hasn't been invaded by women. But I understand that the 38th decided to set it up in one of their heads and claim the distinction of being the only battalion equipped with a sure-enough, honest-to-God bidet.

Another amazing piece of equipment attracted my attention at Kiska. It looked so American standing there in the tundra. Machinist Mate first R. G. Halstead, of Kelso, Wash., who was in charge of it, told me it was a complete, self-powered, moving machine shop. Ready to move, it looks something like a truck trailer; but ready for action, it drops its walls, switches on its own power plant, and is ready to repair anything from a watch-spring to a battleship.

Halstead, who worked with a mining outfit in Alaska before the war, listed these machines as part of the unit: lathe, drill press, bench grinder, valve refacing machine, brake re-liner, brake drum truing machine, five-ton arbor press, water distillation unit, welding outfit, compressor and generator. Costing at least $25,000, it is built so that the Seabees can lift it over the side of a ship and set it up on a beach in less than an hour.

"Wouldn't those little slant eyes pop out if they could see this?" Halstead chuckled.

A piece of equipment which every Seabee is proud of is a portable electric refrigerator developed by the Bureau and built by the Hussman-Ligonier Co., of St. Louis. These 150-cubic foot boxes—called "reefers"—contain a gas refrigerating unit which enables them to operate in transit; then they can be assembled as a battery and operate off a central electric generator.

When we entered Kiska Harbor, the 38th had ten tons of fresh boneless steaks, chops and roasts riding in these reefers atop the deck cargo. On the second day after we landed, these boxes had been assembled back of the mess tent and were purring away off the central power plant.

Our first day on the beach, chow was sent to us in twenty-gallon aluminum containers from the ship's kitchens; but on the second day we lined up in the mess tent and loaded bright tin trays with bean soup, Yankee pot roast, browned potatoes, brown gravy, green snap beans, Bartlett pears, bread, butter, and coffee.

Seabee chow is famous on every front. Because Seabees stick to the beaches and because their cooks are experienced and have the finest equipment, the Seabees almost always have hot food. The Army, of course, moving into the hills, must use canned rations, so Army personnel is always welcomed to Seabee chow lines. The Navy has a policy of feeding everybody in the line as long as the food lasts, and at Kiska the 38th served four meals a day to a line which included men from half a dozen Army units, the Amphibious Force and Canadians, as well as its own men.

Food at Kiska was prepared under the direction of Chief Commissary Steward J. H. Mitchell, of Ottumwa, Iowa, a duck-shaped old-time hotel man who served up Army chow at St. Mihiel and in the Argonne.

"It's sure different from the last time,"' he told me. "In France, we were lucky if we could give the boys cold hash. But now we can load these platters down under almost any conditions. Last time we had heavy field ranges that burned wood; we had no portable refrigeration equipment. Now we've got portable stoves that burn flight gasoline; we've got portable reefers; the bone is all out of the meat; and we have the dehydrated foods to fall back on. If I was at the Waldorf, I couldn't serve up any more wholesome food than I can here on this beach at Kiska."

The Jap food was as incomparable to ours as their machines and living conditions. Their storehouses contained sacks of rice and dried beans. For meat they had only canned or dried fish, and for emergency retching purposes I offer you some of that dried squid which they relish.

Were the Seabees disappointed at the Japs having deserted Kiska? The honest answer is no. It might suit the fiction writers better to report that these rugged, hairy-chested construction men stamped their boots and cussed at not getting to kill any Japs. But such an answer would misrepresent the Seabee attitude toward the war.

The Seabee volunteers are skilled men who joined the service because there was a job to do. They want to finish the job and go home. They welcome any break which causes the job to move faster. When the Japs sneaked out of Kiska they allowed us to move in, take advantage of their work, and complete a task within a few days which, against opposition, would have required many weeks and cost plenty of blood.

"Hell, no, I'm not sorry they turned tail," went the general comment. "The more they back up, the thicker they'll get and the easier it will be for us to kill them. The only thing I hate about it is that I worked so damn hard cleaning up my rifle!"

It was on the Kiska trip that I met Doc Stimson (Lieutenant C. A. Stimson, Medical Corps, USNR, Petaluma, Cal.) and heard the story of him and Ito. The story of Doc Stimson and Ito appeared in *The American Mercury* and *Reader's Digest* under the title, "A Jap Discovers America."

I am indebted to the *Mercury* for permission to retell it here. Doc is the medical officer aboard the Navy ship which carried us to Kiska and which, earlier, had carried the Seabees to Attn. Doc understands the Seabees and they understand him, because he worked in lumber camps to pay his way through medical school. He is as friendly as Will Rogers. His eyes sparkle when he talks of his small-town practice which he left after Pearl Harbor; of his own kids back in Petaluma. He thinks people can be pretty swell.

Ordinarily, Doc's sickbay aboard ship is not a busy place. The ship works in the Aleutians, where the weather is cantankerous but healthful. Twice a day, Doc comes in to chat with the two or three mates who are abed and to hear the complaints of others reporting colds or "cat," short for catarrhal fever—the flu of World

War II. The Doc jokes with the fellows quietly; then Kovitz, the chief pharmacist's mate, and McCroskey, pharmacist's mate first class, dole out the oils and pills which are swallowed with profane sputterings.

But when a Red Cross launch comes churning up to the gangway, the sickbay can snap to attention quicker than a Marine boot. The launch will be bringing an emergency aboard. Doc Stimson is suddenly swathed in his whites; the big lights are switched on in the compact operating room; McCroskey is ready with anesthesia; and the whole sickbay sings with efficiency until the emergency is racked up—bathed, bandaged and anointed—between crisp Navy sheets.

There's plenty of America about that sickbay. The corpsmen are as friendly as Doc himself. Kovitz at thirty-eight is already a veteran of twenty years in the Navy. He came from Chicago; the Navy gave him his chance to make magic with medicines. McCroskey is big, blond and youthful, with a smile as broad as his folks' cornfield back in Rudd, Iowa. Dort, who takes temperatures and swabs out, is proud that his old man is police chief at San Diego; and Yeargin, who tends patients and binds fingers, is a lanky redhead from the South.

The show at Attu gave Doc and his corpsmen their big experience. While the Seabees were rattling the bombs, unloading the ship, Doc and his boys pitched in to help the Army with its wounded. The Red Cross launches shuttled between the shore and the ship, and Doc and McCroskey and Dort battled to keep their operating table clear. On the deck, American soldiers lay stoically waiting their turns, and among these Kovitz and Yeargin worked with the wondrous sulfas, plasma and morphine.

After the last desperate fight at Chichagof, the big operating lights burned all night. The men went in pale, muddy and bloody; they came out clean, comforted by the drugs and revived by the blood from the great heart of America.

Then, almost as startling as a torpedo hit, came Ito. The whole ship tightened with surprise; then resentment. Ito was no brother in arms; Ito was the enemy! A contemptible, buck-toothed Enemy who hated America and Americans. Filthy beyond description, he lay sullenly on a Jap stretcher—rough boards nailed on two-by-fours. And, God, he stank! Not any ordinary stench, but a pervading, suffocating stench that made you think of those decaying rats.

An AA gunner looked down from his platform and barked: "For Christ's sake, you dogfaces throw that bastard over the side before he suffocates us all!"

Holding your nose and looking into Ito's face, you could see that he was frightened and in great pain yet determined to betray neither fright nor pain. He and a companion had exhausted their ammunition in a foxhole, and each had held his last grenade against his stomach and pulled the pin. But Ito's gods had let him down. The other Jap's grenade went off, disemboweling him and shattering Ito's leg; but Ito's grenade was a dud. He had lain for days in his own blood and excrement, and now his leg was a greenish, muddy, bloody mass of gas gangrene. Our soldiers had found him still clutching his false grenade.

Ito knew, of course, why the big Americans hadn't bayoneted him. He had told an interpreter. The Americans were bringing him to a special torture machine. They were going to laugh at him, slash off his ears, kick out his teeth, then cut him into a "million-million pieces." Now he lay there on the deck, almost overcome by his pain, yet determined to show these American barbarians how a Jap could die.

What in Heaven's name was to be done with him? Did Kovitz have the right to inject American blood plasma, given freely by some American to save an American's life, into Ito's veins? Did Dort have the right to spend drugs on this Jap carrion? Could Yeargin be expected to bathe this sullen, hateful thing? And, above all, did Doc have the right to devote his operating room, his staff and his own precious skill to this filthy enemy? And what about the actual physical dangers? Gas gangrene is highly infectious. With all the antiseptics, men work over it at considerable risk to themselves.

Were not we in the business of killing Japs, not saving them? Across the bay two destroyers were bouncing like terriers as they blasted at Jap hill positions. A P-38 was diving into mortar nests. Two nights before, drunken Japs had broken through and massacred some of our unarmed medical corpsmen. Shouldn't we, indeed, throw this stinking mess over the side?

I would have wanted time to ponder these questions; to be reassured by some Intelligence officer of the possible value of a

Jap prisoner. But when Doc stepped out of the operating room and saw Ito, he hesitated long enough to ask:

"How about our fellows? Any of them waiting for the operating room?"

"We've caught up for the present, sir," Kovitz replied. "Bring him in," Doc ordered.

Smoothly, the life-salvaging machine went into motion. Kovitz popped a needle into Ito's arm as two seamen passed the stretcher through the door. Off came the filthy uniform and the improvised bandages. On went the hot, soapy water and antiseptic solutions. Dort shot in the blood plasma while McCroskey hunched the Jap far over and probed into his spine with the anesthesia. They strapped Ito to the table; then Doc stepped in to amputate the gangrenous leg.

Up to this point, Ito had remained sullen, contemptuous. But as Doc worked over him, carefully examined his leg to save every possible inch of it, the small, slant eyes began to shift questioningly. The spinal anesthesia had left him conscious, his mind active. His struggle was apparent. He had been so certain that the Americans would torture him. Now he resisted the admission that he was being helped; he was afraid to recognize that his whole training had been a lie. His lips quivered. Perspiration poured from his face. His eyes jumped from McCroskey to Doc. He groped for a word, finally found one.

"A-mer-reek-a! A-mer-reek-a!"

He shouted it several times. He was trying to convince himself of an unbelievable discovery. Tears streamed from his eyes. He grinned; nodded his head violently up and down.

The operation lasted more than an hour. Doc worked slowly, carefully, halting every few minutes for McCroskey to douse his mask with solution to keep him from being overcome by the stench. He gave Ito the fanciest amputation in the medical books—the type in which a flap of flesh is fashioned and drawn over the end of the leg so that an artificial limb can be worn in comfort.

When they finally unfastened Ito's hands, he grabbed Doc by the arm, sobbed, cried out "A-mer-reek-a," and nodded his head vigorously. Then, like a child saying its prayers, he folded his hands under his chin, and tried to bow several times. Doc looked very tired, smiled at him, and said: "Take him away, boys. And get that leg over the side."

Yeargin weighted the leg, walked out on deck, and heaved it overboard. Then he held to the rail and vomited quietly.

When Ito was brought out of the operating room there was muttering, both among our own wounded and the mates standing by.

"The Doc should have cut it off right up to his chin!"

"I'll bet our fellows at Corregidor got that sort of treatment. Yeah, like hell!"

But the muttering was not against Doc, for when he came out every man on the deck straightened up to attention and felt sort of proud.

After the operation, Ito was given the same care as our own men. By the fourth day he had revived to a point where he was trying to make friends with everyone on the ship. By jabbing furiously enough at his arm, nodding and grinning, he could get one of the corpsmen to give him a shot of morphine. The supply of Hersheys and Planters and Camels he had collected was inexhaustible. Oranges sent him into a spasm of grinning and nodding.

His great disappointment came when he had to leave the ship. They had brought him out on deck and were preparing to swing him over the side before he realized what was happening. Then he began to yell for Doc. When Doc walked up beside the stretcher, Ito grabbed him around the legs, sobbing and yelling. He wanted to go to A-mer-reek-a with Doc. Doc quieted him and sent him on his way to a base prison.

Afterward I sat in Doc's cabin and we talked of Ito. "Well," Doc began, pulling on a cigar, "this is no time for sentimentality. If I had been armed and had come upon Ito in that foxhole, I probably would have bayoneted him. He might have had another, grenade, you know. But the man who found him didn't bayonet him, perhaps for humanitarian reasons, more probably for purely military reasons. Prisoners are often worth great risks. But whatever the reasons, the rules had changed by the time Ito reached the ship's deck. He was a human being in pain, as well as a prisoner of war with certain rights we respect, and the Navy could do nothing less than give him the best we had."

"What about the operation?" I asked. "Did you do as careful a job on Ito as you would have done on an American?"

He answered without hesitation. "Certainly. There can be no degree in a medical man's efforts, once he has turned his hand toward saving a human life. You can't say, 'I tried harder to save this man than that one.' You can only do your best. Being human, I'd naturally feel more emotional over one of our own—but degrees of effort? Of course not. I couldn't have worked more carefully on the Captain than I did on that Jap."

"Do you see any reason for hope in Ito's reaction?" I asked.

This time he hesitated. "Yes," he replied slowly, "but only if we have a clear understanding of the experience. Our first consideration in handling Ito was military. A soldier risked his life to take Ito prisoner. My corpsmen and I risked infection to save him. We did this, first, because of Ito's possible military value to us. Enlightened selfishness was the second consideration. If Ito's stinking body was to stay aboard our ship, we had to cut off some of it, then clean up the rest of it and restore it to health. We had to do this for our own sake as well as Ito's. Our third and last consideration was humanitarian, and I'd say that Ito's obvious effort to show his gratitude is a hopeful sign.

"I think we should proceed against the Jap people in the same manner. We should kill off the most diseased portion. Then, because we must live in the same world with them, we must help to restore the remainder to physical and mental health. And, finally, we should show ourselves the humanitarians that we are and hope that the whole Jap reaction will be the same as Ito's."

Twenty-five thousand Seabees, along with many thousands of Army Engineers, have toiled along the Seattle-Attu road. They have done more than build a military highway; they have built a modern world where nothing existed before.

CB machine gun crew

(133 CB Hq Security platoon)

11: The Stevedore Battalions

MODERN CARGO HANDLING IS NO LONGER a job for men with strong backs and weak minds. The old picture of a line of singing huskies marching along the levee and up the gangway with sacks on their shoulders belongs to romance. It isn't done that way anymore. Modern stevedoring is done with machines by quick-thinking, trained, agile and willing men.

In the fall of 1942, it became apparent that the Navy would be forced to organize special battalions of stevedores to handle the mountains of freight which had to flow over open beaches in the Pacific. The nature of the Pacific war made stevedoring at the advance bases as hazardous and difficult as construction. An unloading ship was a prime target for the enemy. Then, all the normal difficulties of unloading were multiplied by the absence of piers in the forward islands.

We had no piers for two reasons: there had been no time to build them; and until an island is made secure from enemy attack it is foolish to build piers, since they will only be destroyed by enemy bombs. This meant that when a freighter arrived at a place like Guadalcanal, she had to anchor offshore and unload her cargo onto heaving barges; then the barges ran to the beach, where the cargo had to be handled again onto trucks. This ship-to-shore process doubled the normal amount of stevedoring.

Even granting that civilian ship's crews were willing to risk bombs and willing to work round the clock in drenching rains, additional stevedoring forces were necessary. Shipping space was short; the supply lines were long and tenuous; it was imperative that ships be unloaded and turned around quickly at their destinations. At one time in 1942, eighty-three ships were lying at anchor in the South Pacific waiting to be unloaded.

The Navy needed stevedores and, as with the construction men, it seemed wise for the stevedores to be members of the armed forces, trained to fight as well as work, and subject to military discipline. Where a battle may turn on the handling of one cargo under fire, it seemed unwise for all the armed contingents in an area to be dependent on the whims of a civilian crew.

When the ship unloading situation was at its worst in the South Pacific, a Construction Battalion was put to work unloading ships. Amazingly, though only a few men in the battalion were experienced cargo handlers, the Seabees were able to unload freighters twice as fast as the civilian crews had been unloading them. The Seabees more than made up in enthusiasm what they lacked in experience. They were willing to forget the clock and damn the weather.

The result was so encouraging that the Navy insisted on the Civil Engineers Corps' organizing the stevedore battalions. A total of thirty battalions (about 30,000 officers and men) were authorized for this work.

The CEC designated the stevedore battalions "Special" battalions and rushed plans for their creation. As with the first construction battalions, the need was so urgent that there was little time to train the first "Specials." We had moved into Guadalcanal, and if that battle was to be won we had to have men who would stick with those ships and unload them in spite of bombs, shells and weather.

To form the First Special Battalion, the CEC simply grabbed 95 men with stevedoring experience who had enlisted for service with the construction battalions, added 900-odd others who knew something about rigging and handling barges and small boats, and rushed the group to the Pacific where they were joined by the Second, Third, and Fourth Specials.

These four battalions played a very brave and vital role in turning the tide in the South Pacific. At a time when every ounce of supplies counted, they cleared a bottleneck which threatened to choke our entire effort in that theater. Their enthusiasm was infectious, and even grizzled old freighter masters joined in the applause.

Here is what the master of one transport wrote: "During our emergency departure from Guadalcanal, we found ourselves critically short of men in the engine room. Through the kind cooperation of Lieutenant Curry and his men, we secured seven men who acted as oilers and firemen, who did a most excellent job of helping us in our need."

The master of a Liberty ship wrote: "The manner in which the men of the First Special accepted duty during an attack on us by twelve enemy aircraft was unsurpassed. Gangs were organized as ammunition carriers, magazine loaders, and at fire stations. Some men took positions on the 20-mm guns, some on the 3-inch gun, and some as corpsmen at the First Aid Station."

Another master wrote: "During the course of a raid, while enemy planes were forming for another dive on the ship, the First Specialists calmly removed broken booms and rigging from the hatches and lashed them to the deck for safety. During the night they stood guard watch, relieving the gun crews in order that they might be in best form when needed."

Another skipper wrote: "I wish to inform you that the stevedoring operation aboard this vessel was as fine, if not better, than any civilian stevedoring that I have witnessed in my fifteen years' experience. The cargo was handled carefully and at the same time with maximum dispatch."

As the first terrible emergency eased, the CEC began a training program for the specials. The cargo handling companies were beseeched to give up some of their best men to become officers of the special battalions, and the companies gave splendid cooperation. A nucleus of experienced officers and men was assembled for each battalion, then the construction volunteers who made up the rest of the battalion were trained on shipboard. Two "dry-land Liberty ships" were constructed at Camp Peary to provide training for the inexperienced men.

That this training program has proved successful is indicated by a letter to the officer in charge of the Sixth Special from Captain James E. King, of a Liberty ship.

"I wish to commend the Sixth Special for its performance of duty," Captain King wrote. "On two occasions the Sixth Special has loaded and discharged this vessel. I want to state that they are, without doubt, the finest unit that has ever handled any loading or discharging while I have been in command of this vessel. Their teamwork is really a pleasure to watch, and the amount of cargo discharged per gang per hour is far in excess of any stevedoring done in this area. The stevedores that worked this ship in the States would be put to shame if they could see these boys in action.

"When I look at this battalion, I feel proud to be an American. I have never yet heard one bit of beefing or griping or seen any shirking of duty. Each man seems happy to do his allotted job and does it quickly and efficiently."

The motto of the Seabee specials is "Keep the Hook Moving."

Their indomitable spirit has been caught best by Lieutenant Clemen C. McHale (Chaplains Corps, USNR, Chicago, Ill.) who was attached to the First Special. In a letter to me Chaplain McHale wrote:

"Our war islands in the South Pacific cannot boast of channels, docks and piers, since at Guadalcanal a dock would last only until the next air raid. So, when a ship arrives, it anchors three to five hundred yards offshore and waits for the Seabee stevedores to go into action. For ferry service from ship to shore the stevedores press into service anything that floats. There is a steady stream of ducks, tank lighters and pontoon barges, including 'Big Joe.' 'Big Joe' is the pride of the pontoon fleet, since he is able to take ashore 200 tons at a trip. The most successful barges are the ones made up of three rows of twelve pontoon cells. These have a normal capacity of seventy tons.

"Maneuvering this motley assortment of floats and bringing them alongside a ship in a running sea is a tough job for the Seabee coxswains. The captain will roar: 'Bring that barge alongside Number Three Hatch!' and the coxswain will try to maneuver his barge in between the barges which are already taking cargo from Numbers Two and Four Hatches.

"One captain, watching a young coxswain trying to maneuver his barge in a heavy sea, became exasperated and bellowed: 'Take that damn thing out and anchor it and I'll come alongside!'

"Aboard ship the hatches are open, booms are rigged, winches are in neutral, the Seabee gangs are waiting. As the barge comes alongside, the cargo nets and slings move upward from the holds carrying tons of vital needs. Guns, grenades, serums, plasma, food, fuel, clothing, tobacco, bulldozers and tanks—they all move upward high into the air, then over the side and down to the pitching barge, where the Seabees jump to lash them fast. Back goes the big hook for another load. 'Keep that hook moving!' Once more the winches strain, the booms groan, the cables are taut as bow-strings, and the endless procession increases in cadence as the crews warm up.

"Deep in the hold of the ship, too far down to feel even the whisper of a breeze, but with the tropical sun boiling down, the Seabees are stripped to their waists. Sweat pours in torrents, even filling the men's shoes, but they keep rushing. Always the next lift must be ready when the hook comes back from its journey over the side. Keep that hook moving! There's a war to be won! Our buddies on the beach need this stuff to throw at the Japs!

"The men are accustomed to think in terms of time and more speed, for just over the horizon is the enemy with bomber and submarine. The best defense is speed—put the stuff ashore where it will be safe.

"The barges, with whitecaps licking at their gunnels, creep slowly ashore to be beached as far in as they will go. Then crawler cranes, moving like giant land crabs, creep up alongside, and once again there is that same steady rhythm of swinging hook as the precious cargo is transferred from barge to truck. The barges are needed back at the ship. Keep that hook moving! The trucks are a conveyor belt to the warehouse or, more likely, the open storage area.

"Manpower never hesitates where time can be saved. Anything up to 300 pounds is lifted by hand; men are more easily maneuvered than cranes.

"When the enemy bombers come, the stevedores aboard ship have no time to make the shore. The ship must run, so they stick to her, help to man her guns and to care for her wounded. The greatest air battle of the South Pacific was fought over our stevedores and the ships they were unloading. Ships were hit, and men were swimming everywhere while Jap planes swooped low and strafed them in the water. Where were the stevedores? They were in their small boats, dashing everywhere to rescue men, defying the strafing planes.

"It takes courage to volunteer for perilous posts; and I think it takes more courage to volunteer to work long, weary hours under the simmering heat of a tropical sun. Keeping the supplies rolling in is the monotonous routine of lifting and guiding and watching always for the enemy and sleeping in foxholes. Hours are not counted. I have seen our men work eighteen straight hours in a hatch, then sleep in the hatch to avoid wasting the time necessary to get out and to come back in.

"Nature, too, is the enemy of these men. Even the big tropical moons are dangerous, for then the bombers roam. The winds stir the sea, and the rains cause trucks to bog down. The insects bedevil the men, and the threat of malaria hangs over each man like a shadow. But there is a war to be won! Keep the hook moving!

"During the first three months in the Pacific the First Special handled 112,407 tons of cargo from 33 ships. During this time there were twenty-six air alerts and at least one very serious bombing raid.

"Only one thought lives in the hearts of the men of the First Special. They are proud of the distinction of being first. They are working at the first of the advance bases, and, most of all, they want to remain first in the hearts of the boys on the battle lines.

"The Seabee specials pass both the food and the ammunition. It's their responsibility to 'keep the hook moving.' They are not the sort of Americans who let their fellows down!"

Seabee working with a lift truck

Port Hueneme, California, October 1944

12: Seabee Humor and Ingenuity

WHEN THE SEABEES ARRIVED ON GUADALCANAL for the organization's baptism of fire, they were in a difficult position. In contrast to the Marines whom they were reinforcing, the Seabees lacked all the elements which usually inspire confidence in a military force: superb equipment, training, spit-and-polish, service traditions. The newest branch of the service was being thrown in beside the oldest and proudest; the poorest-trained and equipped beside the best-trained and equipped; the essentially civilian machinist was taking his place alongside the professional fighting man.

Also, the Seabees were "old men" in a "young man's war." Because they must be both skilled and experienced, Seabees are the oldest men in the service. The average age is about 31, and many of the officers and petty officers are veterans of the first World War. The average age of the Army is 27; of the Fleet, 22%; of the Marine Corps, 20%. The Seabees looked like fathers to the 17- and 18-year-old Marines on Guadalcanal.

Watching the Sixth Seabees come ashore, the Marines chortled: "What the hell, pop! Are we running out of men at home already?"

"Say, pop, didn't ya get'cha wars mixed up?"

"Watch ya false teeth, pop. You'll lose 'em when the next bomb goes off."

"So, this is the Seabees! The Confused Bastards! What the hell are you going to do in here?"

It was a difficult moment, but, luckily, American construction men are a thick-skinned variety who can dish it out as well as take it.

"What are we doing here?" the Seabees roared back. "Why, goddamn it, we were sent in here to protect you goddamn Marines!"

That word *protect* saved the day. Nothing, of course, could be more galling to the Marines than the insinuation that they needed protection, so the Seabee had his *raison d'être*. He was the man who "protected the Marines."

By the time the Seabees got ashore the Marines were chuckling: "Never hit a Seabee, for his son might be a Marine." At another island, Seabees stamped out "Junior Seabee" buttons which they announced would be given to Marines who had put in enough months of service to prove they were worthy of the "honor."

During the early fighting on Guadalcanal, the tanks had one woeful weakness: an open sprocket over which the tread revolved. A Jap could leap out, jam a crowbar through the spokes of the sprocket, and stop the tank dead. A Seabee machinist took one look and provided a remedy in twenty minutes. He cut the top out of a fuel drum with a torch, welded the circular piece over the sprocket so that the crowbar couldn't slip between the spokes, then walked away muttering something about having to "protect these helpless Marines."

Far from being deplorable, this intra-service razzing is one of the strengths of Americans at war. It's our way of building team spirit; of combating tension and boredom. It's the Giant-Dodger or Georgia-Georgia Tech feud staged deliberately to provide purpose and relief. Pride-of-outfit is an essential in wartime; it gives a guy something to fight for—a simple, easily understood reason for carrying on. Four Freedoms and Atlantic Charters are forensic stuff; what drives men through muddy death is pride-of-outfit. The Seabees have built their pride-of-outfit on "Can Do"; on their ingenuity; on being the world's finest war builders; and on being "the goddamnedest, toughest road gang in history." Seabees are the men amongst the boys. Marines only capture territory; it's the Seabees who improve territory.

As soon as the Seabees had watched the Marines clean out a Jap rat nest, and as soon as the Marines had watched the Seabees operate under bombs and shells on Henderson Field, each outfit knew that the other was good enough to play on his team. Seabee battalions became integral parts of Marine combat divisions. Marine combat reporters became the warmest journalistic friends of the Seabees. Seabees and Marines became natural allies in the ancient feud between men in the Navy who operate ships and those who do not. Marines and Seabees stand at one end of the bar, the "sailors" at the other end. The "Fleet Navy" is on one side; the "shore Navy" on the other. But when no third parties are around, Seabees and Marines wrangle over which out-fit is the toughest, which one is winning the war.

The sharpest banter concerns the jealously guarded Marine prerogative for always getting everywhere first. For years, Marine poets have been proclaiming that when the Army and Navy get to Heaven they will find Marines guarding the streets. Now the brash Seabee poets insist that when the Marines get to Heaven they will find that Seabees have built the streets! And the argument as to who will get to Tokyo first grows louder and lustier by the hour.

The Seabees pounced on an incident at New Georgia Island and rubbed it mercilessly into Marine hide. In July,1943, during the Munda operation, a Marine detachment made the classic dawn assault on a New Georgia beach. As they came tearing up on the beach looking for Japs, a party of white men stepped out from behind trees and waved to them. Marine jaws dropped as the party approached and Seabee Lieutenant Bob Ryan, of Santa Paula, Cal., extended his hand to the Marine major.

"Major, the Seabees are always happy to welcome the Marines!" Lieutenant Ryan said warmly, with a heavy tongue in his cheek. Then a Seabee boatswain's mate walked over, clapped a Marine private on the back and quipped: "What kept yuh, bud?" The quip was almost too much for a self-respecting Marine to take. Great oaths rent the air and there was much stamping of earth before the Montezuma Boys got around to appreciating the Seabee jest.

Lieutenant Ryan's party had been scouting for an airstrip location when they spied the Marines approaching. The Marines insisted that the whole affair was a frame-up, but the Seabees contend that it is typical of the manner in which they must "protect the Marines."

An example of the lush efforts of the Seabee poets are these quatrains:

We work like hell, we fight like hell,
And always come back for more:
The Navy's advance base engineers
On many a foreign shore.

On half the lousy islands

From here to Timbuktu,
You'll find a hive of Seabees,
One hell of a fighting crew.

The admiral just dropped around
To chat the other night,
He said, "Now boys, I know you work,
But you've also been trained to fight.

"So, if there's any trouble, don't stop
To put on your jeans;
Just drop your tools, grab up your guns
And protect those poor marines!
- Anonymous

To support their claim to be the toughest, don't-give-a-damnedest outfit in the service, the Seabees have accumulated many stories, both factual and apocryphal.

On a certain Pacific island, it is said, natives were mopping up the remaining Japs. One day a group of natives wiped out a party of Japs, but the natives hesitated to kill a strange animal which the Japs had brought to the island. The animal was a goat, and after observing the goat curiously, the natives returned to their chief for instructions as to whether or not they should kill the strange beast.

"What manner of beast is it?" the chief asked.

"Oh, he's very strange, majesty," the natives replied. "He has fierce eyes, long horns, a shaggy beard, will eat anything, and stinks like hell."

"Spare him," the chief ruled at once. "Don't kill him. He's what the Americans call a Seabee."

While this story may be apocryphal, it is a fact that several Seabee battalions have billy goats as mascots. Most famous of these goats is Isa, a lordly, bellicose veteran of many bombing raids and shellings, who is mascot of the 37th Battalion. Attired in Navy blue blouse emblazoned with Seabee insignia, Isa struts up gangways behind his keeper, Robert Caddell, Chief Boatswain's Mate, Washington, D.C., Isa and the other goats have learned to hit foxholes in a hurry and escape Jap fire, but they are constantly threatened by the "friendly" fire of Army and

Marine snipers in quest of fresh meat. One of the bloodiest pitched battles of the South Pacific was fought between a Seabee battalion and an Army detachment after a Seabee goat had embellished Army chow.

Marines and soldiers collect ordinary souvenirs; the Seabees prefer their souvenirs with Japs attached. Two Seabees, both from St. Louis, O. F. Maly, Seaman first, and A. B. Banjai, Shipfitter third, went out one afternoon looking for souvenirs. On a hill just beyond camp limits they ran smack into two Jap soldiers armed with rifles and an axe. The two unarmed Seabees went into action. They killed one Jap by smashing him over the head with his own gun butt, then shot the other Jap down as he ran away. They brought the souvenirs—and the Japs—back into camp.

Seabee Carl E. Hull is a 46-year-old former policeman of San Pedro, Cal. During operations at Torokina Point on Bougainville, Hull captured a Jap soldier, although he himself was armed only with an axe. In presenting him the Silver Star, Admiral Halsey described Hull as the "hatchet-packing member of the jungle-hacking, Jap-cracking all-American team."

Herbert R. Wagner, Machinist's Mate third, Columbus, Ohio, provided proof that Seabees kill Japs "before breakfast." On his way to the galley for duty at 0400, Wagner stumbled into a Jap soldier in the darkness. He hit the Jap with a flying tackle, cracked him over the skull with a rock, and gouged his eyes until the Nip screamed surrender. The Jap had cut Wagner on the arms with a bayonet, but as soon as these cuts were taped up, Wagner continued on to the galley.

In the Treasury Islands, October 27, 1943, Aurelio Tassone, Machinist's Mate first, Milford, Mass., came ashore on a twenty-ton bulldozer and found that a Jap pillbox was holding up the advance. Tassone raised his big blade like a shield, drove his big machine toward the coconut-logged bunker. At the proper instant he dropped the blade, smashed the bunker and filled it with tons of earth. Later, twelve Jap bodies were found in the bunker.

Coldest blooded of all Seabees are the members of the demolition units. They are "hard-rock men," as nerveless as clams, who carry TNT and Bangalore torpedoes into an enemy-held harbor and blast out obstructions to a landing. They are the real advance agents of amphibious warfare.

Details of this activity add up to a nightmare. Since most of the work is done in pitch darkness, the men must depend entirely on their sense of feel. The obstructions are underwater, so the men wear various types of diving gear, depending on the depth. On a typical mission the unit—one officer and five men—will sneak toward a beach at night, slip over the side of their small boat and begin exploring channels, feeling for obstructions. The enemy is as ingenious underwater as he is on land. He drives "horn scullies"—sharpened rails which will rip the bottom out of any boat; he sinks barges to clog channels, then strings underwater barbed wire and lays booby traps around the obstruction to "protect" it from demolition crews.

The Seabees feel carefully for the booby traps and remove them. They cut the barbed wire with underwater torches or blow it with Bangalores. Finally, they blast the obstruction with TNT, clearing the channel. Or their assignment may be a simpler one, such as cutting a new channel through a sandbar or "coaxing" an LST off a beach. Sometimes the sand will settle around an LST and form a suction so strong that the ship can't be pulled off. The Seabees know how to place explosive charges so that the explosions will break the suction and enable tugs to extricate the ship.

Since a single wrong move by any one of the five members can wipe out the entire demolition unit, mutual confidence within a unit is imperative. So, the units are formed with great care. The men live together, train together, work together; and only in rare circumstances is the personnel of a unit changed.

Lieutenant Fred A. Wise (CEC, USNR, Reno, Nev.) led the most successful unit in the Sicilian invasion. After the landing his unit joined the Army Engineers and went after landmines and boobies. It was during this operation that Seaman Theodore (Johnny) South, of Marion, Ill., established his reputation for being able to "smell any mine the Germans can lay." Disdaining the "carpet sweeper"—the mechanical searching device—South digs for landmines "by smell alone."

A report from Tulagi is another bit of Seabee lore. The report was sent to me by Lieutenant Paul A. Rossiter (CEC, USNR, Clear Lake, Iowa): "The lumbering platoons of the 27th Battalion are winning the battle for lumber in the Solomons. We have found that the mangrove and dingally trees are excellent for piling, wharf decking and warehouse flooring. They are dense, heavy timbers, highly resistant to teredos and termites. But logging this timber is a job which requires tenacity, skill and high courage.

"Both of these trees grow in swamps filled with brackish water and dense undergrowth. Their roots join the trees frequently eight or ten feet above the swamps, and these tangled roots grow up from the swamp and back down, forming ubiquitous knees which make working difficult. The men felling these trees must work knee-deep in ooze and water all day, and must watch out for crocodiles, which they fight off with their axes. The men suffer from fungus infections of the feet, and there are poisonous vines which cause an extremely painful rash resembling poison ivy. The sap of the bole tree causes a similar rash. To treat these infections, we apply calamine lotion and require the patient to remain naked and try not to perspire, since perspiration spreads the infection.

"Although this work is extremely distasteful and is being performed by skilled men who could command very high wages at home, our crews have worked continuously for five-week stretches without complaining."

These examples of Seabee activity are not extraordinary. They are simply a part of the support for the Seabee claim to "toughness."

There are so many legendary examples of Seabee ingenuity that only a representative group can be included here.

Warrant Officer Robert C. Straub (CEC, USNR, Charleston, S.C.) may have affected the whole course of the war in the South Pacific. In the early days at Espiritu Santo the direst need was for machine tools to make new parts for trucks, and heavy grading equipment. One precious shipment of these tools was lost en route from the States. Straub had an idea. He had once been a West Coast machinery salesman, and some of his customers had been New Zealanders. He hopped a plane and headed for New Zealand on a scouting expedition.

"Naturally, I had no list of my former customers," he related, "so I had to work from memory. As soon as I located one customer, he would help me find others. In a few days, I found most of those people, and luckily, they still had the machines I had sold them. Moreover, the machines were idle because of the lack of materials down there.

"I had to get Government permission to take the machines out of the country. Then I had to find some way to pay for them. A Navy Supply Corps captain came to my rescue by arranging to obtain the machines through reverse Lend-Lease. We got a ship and rushed the whole load of precious tools to the Solomons. We had milling machines, lathes and welding equipment.

"The 15th Battalion built a machine shop back in the hills, and we began to trade work for more machines. We made some repairs on the aircraft-carrier *Enterprise*, and the *Enterprise* reciprocated by lending us some more tools. Soon we had to move the shop to larger quarters.

"We tried to keep the shop secret, but soon it became obvious that Seabee equipment kept running while Army and Marine equipment was breaking down. So, we told the other boys about it. They wouldn't believe we had a machine shop at first, then they swamped us with repair work. We even had to start overhauling planes for the Army and the Marines."

Letters from home kept at least one Seabee bulldozer operating in the Ellice Islands. The big machine blew a head gasket, and head gaskets were exactly as plentiful as white women. So, the men gathered their letters from home, laid many layers of paper between thin strips of metal, fitted the improvised gasket into the bulldozer, and put the machine back into action.

When a condenser blew out in Samoa, Paul B. Phillips (Chief Carpenter's Mate, Long Beach, Cal.) was equal to the emergency. With tinfoil collected from cigarette packs, some waxed paper taken from a fruitcake package, and a flat iron, Phillips rolled out alternating layers of tinfoil and waxed paper, stuffed it into a discarded beer can, and his engine was running again.

American engineers all over the world now know how to improvise jeep and truck radiators out of our metal ammunition cases. The man who did it first was Harold A. Duvall, Fireman first, Erie, Mich., who kept captured Jap trucks operating on Guadalcanal. Other Seabees have kept tractors operating by mounting a fuel drum in place of a smashed radiator.

These fifty-gallon fuel drums, in fact, are staple material for Seabee improvisation. Most important, the Seabees cutout the heads, weld the drums together and make culverts of them. Miles of such culverts have been laid along the roads to Tokyo. Also, the drums are used extensively for roofing, and one group of

Seabees fashioned a sightseeing canoe from six drums, using Jap seaplane floats for outrigging.

Coral chews up truck tires very quickly. When the tires will no longer hold air-filled tubes, the Seabees fill them with a mixture of palm tree sawdust and cement and get hundreds of extra miles of wear. Beer and Coco-Cola bottles are pressed into service: they make excellent insulators for power and communication lines.

Seabee ingenuity, too, has had its lighter side. In Algiers, the 120th Battalion planned a mighty Christmas celebration for the French and Arab kids; The men wanted to paint dolls at night, but they lacked the delicate paintbrushes necessary for such work. Frank Weideman, Carpenter's Mate third, Minneapolis, Minn., who is part Chippewa Indian, found the answer. He chased down three cats, plucked their hair from their backs, and made the necessary paintbrushes. In private life, Weideman is a forester and plucking hair or feathers from live animals is old stuff to him. He makes all of his own flies for fishing by plucking feathers from birds. With the improvised brushes, the men of the 120th painted 3,000 wooden toys for the kids' Christmas. Sam Todd, Machinist's Mate first, Tuscaloosa, Ala., added his touch to this Christmas celebration by forging a set of beer spigots.

The Seabees have drunk every conceivable alcoholic concoction in the world, and they have improvised a few new ones. While the Zombie was in its heyday in New York, Seabees in the Aleutians were mixing "Dehorns"—a sure cure for loneliness. The explosive ingredient in a Dehorn is the colorless liquid that is used to thin camouflage paint. Just what the chemical composition of paint-thinner is, no one seems to know—or care—but if you will add three fingers of paint-thinner to a small bottle of beer, you'll get a Dehorn that will blast the top of your head off.

The Seabees learned from the Polynesians how to put nature to work. If you will drill a hole in a fresh coconut, fill said coconut with raisins, close the hole, bury the coconut in the ground for five days, then dig up and serve—you have a cure for all human ills, including homesickness.

In our amphibious tanks—the indomitable "amphtrack" which made possible our landing on Tarawa—the gasoline tanks are made of copper. They also contain an incredible amount of copper tubing. Young, naive Marines had been in possession of this knowledge for months and had made nothing of it. Then the more experienced and ingenious Seabees opened their eyes. If you will salvage this copper, cut the top off the tank with a torch, rig the tubing properly, put in the proper mixture of chopped sugar cane, you can eventually create a most potable batch of—molasses.

The Seabee commissary stewards are as ingenious as the rest. All of them are old timers around construction camps, and they are the best camouflages of Spam in the service. In the lean days on Guadalcanal, Ben C. Rudder, Chief Commissary Steward, San Francisco, carved a niche for himself in Seabee and Marine memories. Rudder had Jap rice, corned-willie and canned frankfurters to experiment with, but he struggled valiantly. He served boiled rice, rice pudding, chili and rice, tomatoes and rice, and rice with raisins. There were a few native cattle on the island, but the men had been ordered not to molest these cattle. Strangely, however, Rudder went out one day and was viciously attacked by a cow. That night there was hamburger for dinner. A ruling came down that all native cattle hit by shell fragments would be officially available for chow. After this, the mortality among the cows was staggering.

Nor was this a singular occurrence. In British Samoa, a New Zealand plantation owner had many cows, but they were not available to Seabees. However, if a cow lumbered out in front of a truck—well, we could only charge her up to Lend-Lease and make steak out of her. As ingenious as the Seabees are, they could never teach those cows to stay off the roads. Indeed, on more than one occasion, trucks veered off the road and were un-fortunate enough to crash into a cow.

After the fall of Bizerte, the 120th Battalion enjoyed the biggest Seabee feast of the war. In Algiers Lieutenant M. A. Walker (CEC, USNR, Lexington, Ky.) organized a hunting party, traveled forty miles to an Arab village, and obtained native guides for a boar hunt. The party killed seven big boars—roughly 2100 pounds of meat—and brought them back for a battalion barbe-cue. Beer-and-boar, the 120th reports, is a most welcome relief from Spam.

The only place in the Pacific where you can get honey and hot biscuit for breakfast is at the Third Special Battalion's chow hall at Espiritu Santo. While on a scouting trip in the jungle, W.

A. Lundy, Electrician's Mate second, Brewton, Ala., and H. W. Robarge, Boatswain's Mate first, Chicago, Ill., found several large colonies of wild bees. The Seabees conscripted the honey bees, and now the bees are hard at work in American hives.

Accidents to dental plates, spectacles and watches can be annoying and even tragic on jungle islands. The Seabees have perfected a method for welding dental plates: they use a mixture of ground rubber and ordinary cement and leave the dental plate in a carpenter's vise overnight. In all the war zones there are hundreds of watch crystals made by Seabees out of the plexiglass from wrecked planes. And one Army brigadier-general figuratively owes his rank to a Seabee machinist. When the general was promoted from a colonel, there were no silver stars within a thousand miles. The Seabee fashioned two stars out of two quarters so that the general could besport himself properly.

13: The "Ring Around Rabaul"

AUGUST IS THE FATEFUL MONTH IN OUR Pacific operations. On August 7, 1942, the invasion of Guadalcanal began. Then followed almost a year of sea, air and ground fighting—and furious construction by the Seabees and other engineering units. The issue hung in the balance. Would we stop the Japs and slowly move to the offensive ourselves, or would the Japs throw us out and resume their offensive? Five Naval battles were fought. We were seven months driving the last Jap off the ninety-mile long island. Slowly, the character of our air war changed from desperate defense to heavy offense; our fighter strips were changed into bomber strips. And slowly and just as decisively, the Seabees converted Guadalcanal from a jungle into a modern and powerful island base.

On June 30, 1943, nineteen months after Pearl Harbor, the tide had turned. We began to move northward. We landed on Rendova and New Georgia, as detailed in Chapter 2, and captured the big Jap airdrome at Munda. Seabee battalions moved in, opened the Munda strips to our planes on August 14, and subsequently made Munda, "one of the most powerful air bases in the South Pacific." But we had no intention of stopping at Munda. You will recall that the Seabees had been ordered to have the Munda strips in operation not later than August 18. The reason will now become apparent.

Our next objective above Munda was the island of Vella Lavella. We needed a fighter strip on Vella Lavella from which fighter planes could join our bombers from Munda and escort them over all the targets on Bougainville. But before we could begin construction on Vella Lavella, the Munda strips had to be in operation so that fighters from Munda could cover the Seabees landing on Vella Lavella. This is the perfect "book" illustration of how planes are dependent upon construction and of how construction is dependent upon fighter planes.

The fighter strip must always be the most forward construction objective. Yet, in the presence of enemy planes, this construction will need fighter cover, else your construction party and their installations will catch hell such as the 24th Battalion suffered at Rendova. Thus, the Seabee landing on Vella Lavella was planned to coincide with our opening of the Munda strips so that fighters from Munda could protect the Seabees on Vella Lavella from Jap planes coming from Bougainville.

On August 11, 1943, while the 24th and 73rd Seabee Battalions were rushing repairs on the newly-captured Munda strips, the 58th Battalion prepared to embark from Guadalcanal for the landing on Vella Lavella. An advance party of the 58th was to go ahead, survey the site for the airstrip, and mark the beach for the landing operation.

This party included Lieutenant John L. Reynolds (CEC, USNR, Eugene, Ore.); Lieutenant (jg) Richard A. Currie (CEC, USNR, Jefferson City, Mo.); Warrant Officer Roy H. Smith (CEC, USNR, Oakland, Cal.); Chief Carpenter's Mate William H. Moss, Johnston, Pa.; and Chief Carpenter's Mate Francis J. Dowling, Washington, Pa.

The scouting party boarded PT boats at Guadalcanal on the afternoon of August 11 for the overnight run up to Vella Lavella. It was a rough trip. Not only did the party suffer the agonies of PT seasickness, but Jap planes spotted the wakes of the boats and bombed and strafed them for two hours.

Lieutenant Reynolds reported: "There was nothing for us to do but lie under the torpedo tubes and pray. For a while we prayed for the bombs not to hit us; then, as the seasick-ness grew unbearable, we prayed for the bombs to hit us. But, fortunately for the expedition, none of us were hurt."

The party sneaked ashore on Vella Lavella just before daylight on August 12. The island was alive with Jap patrols, but in their best Indian fashion the officers began surveying the landing and airstrip sites. On the thirteenth, seeing that they were certain to be discovered by a Jap patrol, they ambushed the patrol and wiped it out to the last man.

"We taught those Japs a few jungle tricks," Lieutenant Reynolds said, "but the next thirty-six hours were uneasy ones for us. We had to dodge even larger patrols, and our men coming into land on the fifteenth certainly looked good to us.

However, while the scouting party was ambushing Japs, the main landing party was having troubles of its own. The first detachment of the 58th Battalion and the Army's 35th Infantry Combat Team had boarded two LCI's and two LST's at Koli Point on August 13. On the night of the thirteenth the craft were lying off Lunga Point when Jap planes attacked them.

Planes came in at low altitude dropping flares, then dive-bombers and strafing planes followed. The attack lasted for three hours, but it was beaten off without serious damage. The convoy shoved off on the fourteenth and at dawn on the fifteenth, it was approaching the beach at Vella Lavella.

It was a beautiful sight. The tropical green of the island was framed in the blue of sea and sky. Everything was quiet, and the sun was coming up in a burst of gold. The Army boys hit the beach at 0600, met little opposition and swept on inland. The Seabees followed closely, and were unloading the LCI's at Bara-oma Village at 0735. B.A.R. men were acting as guards, and the unloading proceeded swiftly because it had been rehearsed many times at Guadalcanal. After about twenty minutes, however, when the LCT's were practically unloaded, all hell broke loose. Every gun on the ships began firing, but planes seemed to be screaming down from all sides. The attack lasted five minutes; then, a few minutes later, it began again. Through some miracle none of the Seabees were wounded.

When the attack was over, Seabees began unloading the LST's. The D-8 bulldozers were brought off and began cutting roads into the jungle to the areas chosen for supply dumps. There were three more bombing attacks during the day, but the ships were unloaded, and the Seabees moved 500 yards inland and dug foxholes. That night there were thirteen more bombing and strafing attacks, and by morning there were a number of psycho-neurotics. However, the men pitched in with great enthu-siasm to move the supplies to safety. There were so many attacks and alerts that it was practically "Condition Red" all day.

The second wave came in at 1800 on August 17. Bringing in the ships at this hour seemed a mistake, since there was no air cover from Munda this late in the afternoon. The only defense against air attacks was anti-aircraft guns. Attempts were made to unload the ships, but the constant attacks made unloading im-possible. The three LST's retracted, and one of them was hit and destroyed. The battalion lost two trucks, two carryalls, and most of their tents and cots on this ship. Next day the two remaining LST's were unloaded.

The third wave arrived on August 22. While unloading these two LST's, there were two severe bombings, and three men were killed and five wounded. All of the casualties were assisting in the manning of guns on the LST's. The dead were: Eric A. Breiby, Carpenter's Mate third, Palisades Park, N.J.; Walter F. Busby, Gunners Mate third, North Adams, Mass.; and Robert F. Newman, Carpenter's Mate third, New Hyde Park, N.Y.

The fourth wave arrived on August 26 and the fifth on August 31. By this time the enemy air attacks had virtually ceased, due to the heavy cover of fighters furnished from Munda.

On October 27, 1943, a detachment of the 87th Seabees Battalion landed on Mono in the Treasury Islands, which are north and west of Vella Lavella. The detachment was commanded by Lieutenant Charles E. Turnbull (CEC, USNR, Raleigh, N.C.), and it brought distinction to Aurelio Tassone, a 28-year old Machinist's Mate first, of Milford, Mass.

The landing party had no tanks, but the Seabees had landed four bulldozers to begin clearing operations. One stubborn Jap pillbox was holding up the landing. Tassone maneuvered his bulldozer to a difficult angle of fire for the Japs, then while Lieutenant Turnbull lay in the open and fired at the apertures in the pillbox, Tassone started a run for the Japs.

"The big machine moved slowly toward the pillbox," Lieutenant Turnbull reported, "because Tassone insisted on running in low gear so that he would have power enough to crash the pillbox. He couldn't run in high gear and then shift to low gear, since that would mean bringing the bulldozer to a dead stop before the pillbox. He simply raised the blade and rolled ponderously forward. Jap machine-gun fire rattled off the blade, and it seemed that Tassone would be hit at any moment."

At the proper second, Tassone dropped his blade and literally buried the pillbox under a ton of earth.

After the island had been occupied, men of the 87th dug into the smashed pillbox and found the bodies of twelve Japs. Tassone, a slight, serious Italian-American, was awarded the Silver Star.

The 87th completed the airstrip in the Treasuries early in November, and it has been instrumental in the reduction of Rabaul.

On November 1, 1943, a detachment of the 75th Seabee Battalion landed with the first wave of Marines at Torokina Point,

Bougainville. The operation is described by Lieutenant (jg) Robert E. Johnson (CEC, USNR, Charleston, W. Va.), who commanded the detachment.

"The five officers and ninety-five men who composed our landing detachment were all volunteers," Lieutenant Johnson reported. "We came in with the Marines on the USS President Adams; and for the landing, we divided ourselves into four units—one to unload ammunition; another to unload fuel; another to unload rations and packs; and the fourth Seabee unit manned the machine guns on all Higgins boats and tank lighters.

"We were to follow ashore immediately behind Company C, First Battalion, Third Marine Division, which was the only assault force expected to meet any opposition. At 0545 on D-Day, we went over the side and began our run for the beach. Our landing craft were ordered to pass through the narrow channel between Puruata and Torokina Islands. The Japs had machinegun nests on the inside of both islands, and they fired heavily on our first assault boats. Jap planes also strafed us on the run-in. Our Seabee gunners made those Jap machine guns ineffective and helped to drive off the Zeros. One landing craft was hit by artillery fire, and we had to unload the wounded from it under rather desperate conditions.

"At the beach we encountered determined resistance. The 250 Marines and the 100 Seabees worked perfectly as a team. The Seabee gunners provided cover while the Marines advanced to erase the Japs with grenades and flamethrowers. When a Marine was shot from a crippled tractor which was pulling in the first load of ammunition, a Seabee leaped to his place, repaired the tractor, and delivered the ammunition.

"The Seabees dug foxholes not only for themselves but also for the Marines and for all casualties who were unable to dig their own. When a group of Marines was about to be wiped out because of lack of supplies, three Seabees managed to get through with ammunition and to bring back the wounded. Our medical officer and his corpsmen moved in to treat the front-line wounded and to handle Graves Registration.

"The first Seabee to be killed was Harry Edward Webb, Boatswain's Mate second, St. Louis, Mo. A Jap sniper caught him while he was helping to man the line of beach which the Seabees had been assigned to defend. We got the sniper.

"Our Seabee cooks continued to distinguish themselves. Within a few hours after we hit the beach, hot food was served, even to the Marines in the most advanced positions.

"Throughout the operation our officers and men performed their duties with complete disregard for their personal safety."

To begin the construction of the airfields around Empress Augusta Bay, Bougainville, the 71st Battalion began landing on the afternoon of November 1. It was commanded by Commander Austin Brockenbraugh, Jr., of Richmond, Va. There were many difficult construction problems. The ground was swampy, and the rains were unseasonably heavy. Part of the area on which the Torokina fighter strip had to be built was actually beyond our front lines. The Seabees had to risk capture as well as death from enemy fire, and one man was captured by the Japs while he was clearing the strip. A mental hazard for the men was Mt. Bagana, a volcano, which towered near the scene. The Seabees at Bougainville are the only ones who have had to work under an active volcano. In spite of all these handicaps, however, the field was superimposed on the swamp, and planes were operating from it on December 10.

There is a bridge in this area named for Chief Carpenter's Mate Elmer I. Carruthers, Jr., of Charlottesville, Va. A detachment of Seabees under Chief Carruthers was cutting a road in advance of the front lines when the detachment and its Marine security guard was attacked by the Japs. Chief Carruthers and six other men were killed and twenty were wounded, and the entire detachment might have been wiped out had it not been for the gallantry of Chief Carpenter's Mate Joseph R. Bumgarner, of Glenwood, Fla. Bumgarner and a detail were building a bridge when they heard the firing against Carruthers. Bumgarner led his men to the rescue, helped drive off the Japs, and evacuated the Marine and Seabee casualties.

Other Seabee battalions flowed into the Empress Augusta Bay area to convert it into a major base. The Piva bomber strip was built, providing two bomber strips and an additional fighter strip in this area from which to assault Rabaul. In addition to the 71st and 75th Battalions, the 25th, 53rd and 77th Battalions aided in this work.

On February 15, 1944, the _____rd [undisclosed] Seabee Battalion moved even closer to Rabaul by landing with New Zealand assault forces in the Green Islands. The objective was to drive off the Japs and build an airstrip from which fighter planes could give close cover to bombers over Rabaul. It was not a difficult operation. Working around the clock, using floodlights at night and daring the Japs to come over, the battalion completed the airstrip in nineteen days. Several incidents, however, are worthy of the Seabee record.

John Kurtz, Shipfitter first, Whitestone, N.Y., and Joseph C. Havlicek, Shipfitter first, Rocky Point, Long Island, were on duty at the battalion's tank farm when Jap planes struck at the gasoline supply. Shrapnel punctured several of the big tanks, and gasoline began to spurt. Loss of the fuel would have meant the grounding of our planes during a critical period. Disregarding both the Jap planes and the even greater danger of exploding gasoline, Kurtz and Havlicek waded into the fuel and succeeded in plugging the tanks and saving the fuel.

In the same action David Cormier, Shipfitter first, Newton, Mass., was saved from death by James Cirulli, Storekeeper third, West New York, N.J., and Michael Palko, Machinist's Mate second, New York City. Cormier's gasoline-saturated clothes were in flames when Cirulli and Palko reached him. They knocked him down, ripped off their own clothing and used it to snuff the flames. All three suffered severe burns.

The first member of the ____rd to be wounded was the chaplain, Lieutenant William I. Hay (ChC, USNR, Grottoes, Va.). The LST was struck by a bomb going in, and Lieutenant Hay caught one of the fragments. Thomas L. Davis, Carpenter's Mate third, Baltimore, Md., was wounded by the same bomb.

Jose Gonzales Vasquez, Machinist's Mate second, Corpus Christi, Tex., suffered a temporary loss of reputation in the Green Islands. He claims to be the best rifle shot in the battalion. While on guard at an advanced post, Vasquez spotted a running Jap, whipped up his carbine and fired.

"Was I ashamed of myself!" Vasquez reported. "That goddam Jap just kept running."

Vasquez's reputation was restored, however, when he and two other guards followed the Jap into the underbrush, found him dead with a neat hole through his chest.

The eastern half of the circle around Rabaul was completed on March 20, 1944, when the Seabees landed on Emirau Island in the Matthias group. Emirau plugs the escape route from Rabaul to Truk. After the landing on Emirau, Admiral Halsey announced that the campaign in the Solomons had been completed.

While the Seabees were pushing their construction campaign in the Solomons, they were also aiding General MacArthur in New Guinea, New Britain and the Admiralties, and Seabees were in the first wave when our forces landed on Cape Gloucester, New Britain. One of the important links in this campaign was in the Admiralty Islands where a Seabee battalion joined the First Cavalry Division in the storming of Los Negros Island. Repairs to the airstrip were begun while it was still under sniper fire. It is a good, well-located field, only 4000 feet long and it was necessary to lengthen it so that our heavy bombers could take off for the run over Truk.

Seabee casualties at Los Negros were eight men killed; one officer and forty-four men wounded. The dead:

Herbert V. Hufford, Carpenter's Mate first, San Francisco, California; Lorenz Sherman Harris, Carpenter's Mate second, Golden, Colorado; Lloyd Wilson McCaslin, Carpenter's Mate second, Los Angeles, California; Harry August Wiechmann, Chief Ship Fitter, New York, N.Y.; Cecil Raymond Roberts, Jr., Carpenter's Mate second, Billings, Mont.; Robert Dale Hutchins, Coxswain, Klickitat, Wash.; Otis Theodore, Page, Sr., Chief Carpenter's Mate, Los Angeles, California; Thomas W. Milliken, Machinist's Mate third, Woodlawn, Mass.

When the Momote airfield was put into operation, the encirclement of Rabaul was completed. The thousands of Japs still on Bougainville, New Britain and New Ireland were effectively cut off, and General MacArthur was in a position to plan his landings at Hollandia, New Guinea, which would isolate additional thousands of Japs.

For the long, difficult and brilliant campaign which broke the Jap back in the South Pacific, all branches of the service team deserve the highest praise. But it was the Seabees who "built the ring around Rabaul."

14: "Old Faithful" Points for Tokyo

AS THESE LAST WORDS TO THIS ACCOUNT are written, our forces are poised for tremendous, climactic action in both the Atlantic and the Pacific. In the Atlantic, the Seabees have completed their great highways; the big construction job has been done; what lies ahead is a blasting operation to be followed by the unloading of endless ships. When the invasion is launched. The Seabee pontoon detachments will be riding their barges and causeways just as they did at Salerno. Some of them will die—perhaps many of them—but they are the kind of men who don't turn back. Across Navy pontoons will roll the machines which will liberate a continent.

In the Pacific we talk of "the Philippines in '44." There, too, the long roads are nearing completion. In the north, the road from Seattle to Attu is finished; the supplies are stocked and ready; there are enough airfields and docks to service all the sea and air fleets we shall need there. In the central Pacific, the Hawaiian group of islands bristle with every conceivable installation of war. The Gilberts and the Marshalls are ours, and it was the Seabees who helped convert Tarawa, Kwajalein and Eniwetok into bristling naval hedgehogs; into armed filling stations to service the vast one-way parade toward Tokyo.

The 10,000-mile road through the South Pacific has reached up through the Solomons and on out to Hollandia in New Guinea. Ironically, the nearer we get to Japan the easier becomes the task of the Seabees. It's easier to repair an airstrip than it is to build a new one. These American craftsmen who are so superior to the Japs can take advantage of the work which the Japs have done. The faster and farther we go, the more Jap supplies and equipment we capture.

The Philippines and China appear to be the two principal remaining spots where large construction will be needed. Many Seabee battalions may have to be poured into the Philippines, but they will be aided by thousands of willing native workers, many of whom are skilled by American standards. On the China coast, American brain and Chinese brawn will create the plant from which our air and surface fleets can batter the life out of the Japanese monster.

Back down the long roads that they have built, the Seabees can look with the satisfaction of free men who have done a big job voluntarily and well. They are men who have asked little, given much. They have asked only for the privilege of serving their country; for the right to be well led by intelligent and courageous men; for the opportunity of working and staying busy and "getting on with the goddam war." Of all the men in the service, the Seabees are the ones who have the least patience with snafu and tarfu; with delay and incompetence. They are the happiest men in the service when they are at work on purposeful jobs; they are the most rebellious when they are made to feel that they are wasting their time in idleness.

Because the Seabees are civilians with the thinnest veneer of military training, they have been completely free of service jealousy. They have never cared who was working with them or whom they were fighting besides, so long as they were getting on with the job. They have worked beside black men in Africa, brown men in Samoa, white men from Canada, Australia and the British Isles. They have worn Army gear, Navy gear, Marine gear—or native breechcloths—and they have died alongside flyers, sailors and infantrymen. Wherever there has been a gun to pick up or a shovel to put into action, the Seabee has grabbed it and asked no questions.

A few labor unions may have appeared selfish and injudicious on the home front, but the 200,000 union men in the Seabees have impressed every observer with their unselfishness and enthusiasm. The only demand they have made has been for speed and devotion to duty; to "get on with the job so we can go home."

Somewhere in the South Pacific there is a twenty-ton bulldozer called "Old Faithful." It's a battered old monster who has butted down a thousand trees and moved several mountains of earth. A half-dozen Seabee battalions have had "Old Faithful" at one time or other. Six different islands have groaned under the big treads. Scores of Seabee mechanical doctors have tinkered with "Old Faithful" innards, improvised parts and held the monster together with spit and baling wire.

The Seabees have only one request. When they land in Tokyo, they want "Old Faithful" to roll down the ramp of the first landing boat. They want to drive "Old Faithful" through the rubble of Japan's "Fifth Avenue." Then, after they have paraded through Tokyo, the Seabees want to go back down to the beach and welcome the Marines.

Made in the USA
Middletown, DE
03 January 2024

47158367R00094